RJ
506
.M4
B35
1973

Date Due

NOV 8 '89			
FEB 25 '91			
MAR 26 '91			

BRODART, INC.　　Cat. No. 23 233　　Printed in U.S.A.

WITHDRAWN

Isn't It Time He Outgrew This?

or

**A TRAINING PROGRAM
FOR PARENTS
OF RETARDED CHILDREN**

*Isn't It Time He Outgrew This?*
or
A TRAINING PROGRAM FOR PARENTS OF RETARDED CHILDREN

Third Printing

By

VICTOR L. BALDWIN, Ed.D.
H. D. BUD FREDERICKS, Ed.D.
Teaching Research Division
Oregon State System of Higher Education
Monmouth, Oregon

GERRY BRODSKY, M.A.
Mental Health Division
State of Oregon

Illustrations by
Mari VanDyke

CHARLES C THOMAS • PUBLISHER
Springfield • Illinois • U.S.A.

Published and Distributed Throughout the World by
CHARLES C THOMAS • PUBLISHER
BANNERSTONE HOUSE
301-327 East Lawrence Avenue, Springfield, Illinois, U.S.A.

This book is protected by copyright. No part of it may be reproduced in any manner without written permission from the publisher.

© 1973, by CHARLES C THOMAS • PUBLISHER
ISBN 0-398-02626-X
Library of Congress Catalog Card Number: 72-84136

First Printing, 1973
Second Printing, 1976
Third Printing, 1980

With THOMAS BOOKS *careful attention is given to all details of manufacturing and design. It is the Publisher's desire to present books that are satisfactory as to their physical qualities and artistic possibilities and appropriate for their particular use.* THOMAS BOOKS *will be true to those laws of quality that assure a good name and good will.*

Printed in the United States of America

To Timmy Fredericks and hundreds of children like him who have taught us how to teach.

PREFACE

We have attempted to write this book in a manner that would allow us to utilize the information that researchers and practitioners have been discussing in professional journals, while keeping as our major goal that the material be relevant and useful to parents. In order to accomplish this we have had to make many revisions in our original manuscript. Most of the changes were made as a result of direct input from parents who read the material and tried to apply the principles described in the book.

The authors have engaged in several parent-training programs, but a great deal of assistance was provided by other practitioners in the state of Oregon. We would like to especially acknowledge two of these people, Phyllis Fontana of the Corvallis Public School System and Sarolta Nagy of the Mental Health Division. They have used the materials with several parents and have supplied us with many of their own very helpful suggestions.

We have been very fortunate to receive support from various state officials who have been instrumental in encouraging us to continue our parent-training efforts. Specifically, we would like to acknowledge Dr. Mason McQuiston, Director of Special Education, State Board of Education; Mr. James T. McAllister, Director of Title VI, State Board of Education; and Dr. Jerry McGee, Director of Community Mental Retardation Services, Mental Health Division.

We wish to indicate our debt to those in the fields of special education and psychology who have worked with and written books for parents. We have learned much from them and their influence is certainly evident in our own work. We wish to especially acknowledge the work of Dr. Gerry Patterson, *Living With Children*, and the book by Dr. Wes Becker, *Parents Are Teachers*.

We are extremely grateful to the other members of the Exceptional Child Research Program of Teaching Research, Dr. David Grove, Dr. Bill Moore, Mr. John McDonnell, Mr. Ric Crowley, Mr. Bud Moore and Mrs. Katy Rolland for their suggestions, patience and critical comments which have helped us in the production of this book.

The Director of Teaching Research, Dr. James H. Beaird, has provided us with an environment that has been maximally supportive and conducive to the development of our research efforts and the production of this manuscript.

Finally and most importantly we would like to acknowledge the work of Sandy Prater who has typed and retyped drafts of these chapters and suffered through our minor corrections and idiosyncratic behaviors as we have attempted to put this book together. We are eternally grateful to her for her patience and professionalism.

V.L.B.
H.D.F.
G.B.

INTRODUCTION

(To the Professional Engaged
in Parent Training)

NOTE TO PARENTS: Skip this Introduction and read "Introduction for Parents."

THE AUTHORS BEGAN this book as a result of a rather disturbing experience. We found ourselves operating professionally in two different areas. In the first we designed and implemented research projects utilizing rather sophisticated and powerful methods of teaching retarded children. This research was usually done in university clinics, institution settings, and so forth. On the other hand, we were often involved in the training of parents of retarded children. On nearly every occasion we were confronted with the finding that parents and the public in general are completely unaware of techniques now available for teaching the retarded. There seemed to be an enormous "information gap" between the results of research studies (usually written in a language too technical for laymen) and the knowledge or application of those results by parents of retarded children.

The kinds of information that are available to parents usually fall in the two general groups. Some books provide support or moral encouragement to parents of retarded children. They attempt to inform them of the realistic expectations they should have for their children and how to derive as much enjoyment as possible from their children. The second type of book is based upon the kind of research previously mentioned. They often described the theories prevailing in the field and some general notions about reinforcement procedures, social learning, and so on. However, these books at best only give general indications to parents as to how they could teach their child. For the most part they are meant to be used in conjuction with other programs and simply supply information which is felt to be a prerequisite for further teaching of the children.

Our purpose is not to minimize the importance of such books, rather it is to add to them. We believe we have written in understandable language a manual containing specific programs by which parents can develop the types of desired behaviors they wish in their retarded child. The previously mentioned books could well supplement ours. But we do believe that the average parent should be able, if necessary, to use this book alone and stand a good chance of developing specific behavioral programs.

However, the book could also be used to much better advantage in conjuction with organized training programs to supplement the efforts of an individual counselor or teacher. Accordingly, the remainder of this introduction discusses how an individual counselor or teacher can supplement the material presented here or structure training sessions around the material.

First, however, a few explanatory points should be made about some underlying rationale for the book. Although we do believe the book is self-sufficient in the training that it gives parents, nevertheless the eventual success of the programs depends upon how "reinforcing" behavioral change in the child is to the parent. This explains, in part, the emphasis we put upon the measurement of behavior changes. Parents have to learn to recognize the kinds of small changes in behavior they are going to produce on a daily basis. However, we think it crucial that counselors working with parents assess the likelihood that behavioral improvement in the child will be sufficient reinforcement to maintain the parents' interest and cooperation. If the counselor ascertains that this essential ingredient is lacking, then his skill and experience in generating acceptance and understanding of the child should be utilized in sessions with the parents.

The language system we use can easily be criticized, not

only for the particular terms, but also for the apparent sloppiness in their use. We are aware of the present disagreements among behavior modifiers, operant conditioners and precision teachers as to the best available language system. Rather than choose among the competing entries, we chose a language system which emphasized less technical aspects and used terms that seemed to describe more naturally what the parent would be doing. The eventual end in mind is to establish structured training sessions. In most cases, however, it is necessary to eliminate undesirable behaviors or learning deficits before fruitful training begins. Hopefully, a few weeks of behavior modifications would eliminate any barriers to subsequent months or years of training.

It was these considerations that dictated our language system. For example, the word "cue" was used rather than "discriminative stimulus" or "antecedent event" since in training sessions the parents would be instructing or cueing their child in specific ways. We also chose the word "behavior" rather than "response" or "movement," because behavior is a more familiar word. "Reinforcement" was chosen since the word connotes strengthening. We shied away from the use of "acceleration" and "deceleration," and so forth, because the rate measures inherent in these terms would only be incidental in the final analysis. Again our goal is to develop specific complex skills such as shoe-tying, whose base rates (as well as those of most of its component parts) are zero. We are building behaviors from scratch more often than changing their frequency. In addition, the eventual measure of success in skills such as shoe-tying cannot really be translated to the rate of responses per minute.

Of course, this is not true of a behavior which is now occurring at a given rate, such as a behavior problem. . In this situation, the terminology of "acceleration," and so forth, would probably be better suited. However, in trying to use a single language system, we have chosen a system which would better relate to eventual training sessions, then extended it to cover behavior modification.

As a further note, we present only as much "theory" as we

feel necessary to justify to the parents their investment of time and effort in lieu of some chance of success. We did not attempt to make learning theorists of them. Again, our assumption is that if we can get the parents started and attune them to recognizing any progress that might occur, then we assume that the reinforcing properties of the behavior change in their children will maintain the parents' behavior. In addition, other kinds of reinforcers ought to appear as a function of using the program. The ceasing of temper tantrums should lead to a happier household. As the child develops self-sufficient skills, he should become less of a burden to parents and perhaps a good deal more enjoyable.

For the counselor using this book in an outpatient setting, we believe there are particular things that can be done to greatly supplement the program. We suggest that the counselor set up weekly or twice-weekly meetings with parents, either as individuals or in groups, and assign chapters to the parents. All parents should read the first six chapters. Following that, they should be able to individualize the remaining programs to fit their child, contingent upon their behavior analysis of him. Chapters could be assigned, one or two at a time, and in each weekly meeting the reading matter could be discussed with the counselor, leading to a far greater understanding of the principles involved.

We often find that there is a large gap between understanding the principles involved and translating them into workable progams. Once these sessions are underway, the counselor should require parents to produce data (initially base line or assessment data) as soon as possible. These data can not only provide much information to the counselor, but also can provide a topic of discussion and thus some structure for the sessions. We also recommend that each session be made contingent upon the presentation of data. In other words, no data, no session. The data need not be elaborate at first. For example, how often or at what times Johnny throws temper tantrums, or how often Billy wets his pants, are good places to start. We also suggest that as soon as the first few chapters have been read by the parents, you begin to use the new language system. You could begin by translating their ideas or descriptions of behavior into the new language. (This is actually far easier than it might appear. The language system is broad enough to handle any behavior, from bar pressing by a rat to presidential elections.)

The book also indicates which skill or behavior to start with first. Behavior problems, almost by definition, are incompatible with learning sessions and so usually demand first priority. We would, however, caution against the natural tendency for counselors to pick the worst behavior problems to tackle first, and attempt to "sell" the parent right off the bat. Instead, we suggest searching for an easier behavior problem to use as a training vehicle for the parents. A good place to start is a relatively simple behavior which at the present time is not directly and positively reinforced. Case study number 3 in the chapter on behavior problems is the type of which we are speaking. Failing to hang up clothes is not a major behavior problem, but simply one in which neither appropriate nor inappropriate behavior is directly maintained by positive reinforcement. In these simple types of behaviors the counselor should attempt to introduce the concept of the reinforcement of incompatible behavior. This can be done with many simple behaviors by stating the opposite of the behavior problem (picking up clothes rather than throwing them on the floor), and then initiating a program to reinforce only those behaviors. Following successful modification of these behaviors, the counselor can then preceed to more difficult ones.

We also recommend that the counselor consider the use of tangible reinforcers for parents contingent upon their performance. Such things as money or green stamps have been used in these types of programs. Putting "help" on a "business" basis often aids in eliminating any tendencies towards inactivity by the parents. This would seem particularly easy in a clinic where there is a flexible fee charged to the parents dependent upon a yearly income. Thus, it may be practical to return a portion of the fee contingent upon their cooperation in the program. This may be especially vital for parents who are not impressed by the sight of progress in their child. (Patterson has reported use of this technique with success.)

The subsequent chapters suggest analyses to be carried out by the parents and particular hints in developing programs. At times the behavioral analysis will seem to be difficult and time-consuming to parents, but we feel it is a rather crucial component for many of the reasons we have outlined in the chapters. We think a counselor could be especially helpful in this area by assigning, as indicated in the book, various projects involving analysis and measurement.

Parents might well be tempted to skip some of the more demanding, or what seem to be silly assignments from the book. Again, we think these are quite important. Once parents begin training, it should prove helpful for one parent to record evaluations of the other parent's performance as a trainer. A counselor could help devise a measurement system, and aid a parent in evaluating the other parent's use of reinforcements, cues, etc.

One of the more effective training methods we have found could well be used in sessions between counselor and parents. It is often difficult for parents to truly realize that their child is nonverbal, or that he may not have enough language ability or comprehension to be able to respond to the cues that parents are giving them. Parental cues are often confusing and ambiguous and have literal as well as figurative meanings. One training procedure is to have one parent, or initially the counselor, pretend to be a retarded child. The counselor, pretending to be a retarded child, could follow, *literally*, each direction or cue given him. If the counselor can ignore all previous social learning, he can clearly demonstrate to the parents the need for precise cues. For example, if, during the initial session, a parent instructs the counselor-retarded child, "Pick up the shoestring," there is no reason why the counselor should be cooperative and pick up the shoestring using his fingertips. The retarded child is just as likely to pick it up by grasping it with his entire fist. If the counselor is told to "sit down," he should do so at the spot where he is standing. He has not been told to sit in a chair and so he should not look for one to sit upon.

Practice sessions like this can prepare the parent for the kind of unexpected difficulties that may arise when training children, and simultaneously aid the parent in using precise cues and modeling demonstrations for the child.

INTRODUCTION FOR PARENTS

In this book we shall present to you many techniques which are the results of much recent research with the handicapped child. This research has greatly changed the way we look at these children. We no longer believe, for example, that mental and physical handicaps must doom a child to a hopeless and unhappy life. We no longer believe that he cannot master many of the same skills as do other children who are not handicapped. This research also has forced us to reject the notion that a handicapped child who behaves undesirably and unacceptably at times does so *because* he is handicapped.

What we do believe is that his behavior is essentially the same as that of all children; that even undesirable behavior is *learned*, and is not a necessary and unchangeable part of his handicap. If so, if this behavior is really learned, then it can be unlearned the way a new bride "unlearns" her maiden name; or it can be forgotten the same way we forget old telephone numbers and street addresses.

We also look at what a handicapped child *cannot do* from a much different point of view. We no longer say he cannot dress himself because he is handicapped. We say instead, he hasn't *learned* to dress himself yet. The difference is far more than a matter of words, as we hope to show you throughout this book.

The things a handicapped child can and will learn will be learned basically the way all of us have learned. He will learn to tie his shoes or to dress himself, essentially the way we did as children. He will learn to interact and play with other children in the same manner that we did.

In helping him to learn these things, we may accentuate certain aspects of the learning situation so that they stand out

Introduction for Parents

more clearly. We may emphasize certain areas and de-emphasize others. We may take fairly complex behaviors and break them down to small simple ones. Some things we may even have him learn backwards. But, still, in all these things, he will learn essentially the way all of us have learned.

Very often, we shall ask you to continue teaching your child a particular skill after it appears that he has mastered it. We do this because of the results of some very important research. That research looked at what is called "overlearning." Overlearning occurs when we continue for some time to teach a child a task even after he has first mastered it. The research showed that if a mentally handicapped child overlearns a task, he forgets what he has learned as slowly as does a child of normal intelligence. Thus, overlearning seems to somewhat compensate for the slower rate at which handicapped children learn.

What we hope to do in this book is to show you the techniques research has discovered. We will not present this in a way that is technical or confusing: this book is not for scientists; it is for parents of handicapped children. It does not require a Ph.D. or a M.D. to use these methods. It does require what you already possess—interest, dedication and love for your child.

On the other hand, we will not present magical cures. Your child cannot take two of these books overnight and wake up refreshed and healthy the next morning. These methods and techniques work only *if you do*. What the book will do is answer the kinds of questions you probably have been asking yourselves for some time, questions like:

"It seems there's so much he doesn't know, where do I start?" "How do I begin?" This book tells you where and how to begin. It will help you to pinpoint the exact starting place for your child. What we will do is teach *you* how to determine what to do first so that you and your child will not start at a place that is too difficult. Instead, you will start where you both are going to be successful at the very beginning.

"What do I do?" Children are as different as they are alike.

So this book could not be written in one single form for all children. Therefore, it has been designed so that you can tailor-make it to fit you and your child. You can select the behaviors with which you are presently the most concerned. You are then told specifically what to do and how to do it. Each day you will know what goals you will be aiming at and how you can accomplish them. Furthermore, you will know exactly what you are going to do tomorrow. We think that through these techniques we can give you a sense of certainty or sureness about what you are doing.

"*Are we getting anywhere?*" We will show you how to measure the progress you and your child make each day. We will help you to construct visual proof of the success of your efforts. This measurement itself will help to guide you and to determine what you will do at any given moment.

In short, then, we are providing you with prescriptions. But unlike the physician's prescribed pills, more is required of you than just adding water. We can provide the methods, the techniques, the gimmicks, or whatever you need, to teach your child. If you can add the work, hours and dedication, we believe that you can accomplish far more with your child than you may have believed possible.

CONTENTS

Preface vii

Introduction (To the Professional Engaged in Parent Training) ix

Introduction for Parents xvi

Chapter
1. GETTING IT TOGETHER 3
2. BEHAVIOR 11
3. CUES 29
4. REINFORCEMENT 36
5. BEHAVIOR PROBLEMS 47
6. HOW WELL ARE WE DOING? 68
7. SELF-HELP SKILLS 78
8. "USE YOUR SPOON, HARRY!".
   (How to Teach Your Child to Feed Himself) 83
9. "ISN'T IT TIME HE OUTGREW THIS?"
   (Toilet Training Made Easy) 101
10. "ZIP YOUR ZIPPER LIKE A GOOD BOY!"
    (How to Teach Your Child to Dress Himself) 121
11. "WASH YOUR HANDS BEFORE YOU EAT"
    (How to Teach Hygiene Skills) 138
12. Silence Is Not Always Golden
    (HOW DO WE GET HIM TO TALK?) 151
13. Walk, Run, Throw and Catch
    (SPECIAL OLYMPICS, HERE I COME) 161
14. "LOOK MOM, I CAN COUNT"
    (How to Teach Academics) 181
15. "AW MOM, DO I HAVE TO?"
    (How to Set Up a Token System) 195

Index 207

Isn't It Time He Outgrew This?

or

**A TRAINING PROGRAM
FOR PARENTS
OF RETARDED CHILDREN**

Chapter 1

GETTING IT TOGETHER

IN THIS CHAPTER we are going to attempt to supply you with a simple overview of the rationale behind the use of behavior modification techniques and hopefully attempt to provide you with some understanding as to why we have chosen this approach. The techniques and procedures that we are going to discuss throughout this book have been developed over a long period of time and are supported by a great deal of research. We will not attempt to present you with complex research findings and ask you to understand them and compare them against other results that might be available in the literature. Rather, we would like to assure you in the beginning that these techniques have been thoroughly researched and have been highly successful with children who have demonstrated learning problems.

The theory and findings indicate that there is a very close relationship between behavior and environment. In fact, it is this relationship between one's behavior and his environment that these principles thrive upon.

Things that we are going to talk about should not be viewed by you as new and innovative or something that has been recently discovered. The truth is that these principles must have been around from at least the first day of man's existence. The fact that we have only recently been able to explain them and develop a better understanding of man's relationship to his environment contributes to the newness of this approach.

It is obvious to us that you have learned things in your life; your grandparents learned things in their life; and their parents in turn learned many things. It may also be true that none of you and your relatives have had a previous course in behavior modification or are practicing psychology. Mrs. Jones, a first grade teacher, has been getting tremendous behavioral change in children for the past 25 years by interacting with children in her own way. She has probably not been exposed to the scientific principles of the analysis of behavior. Only recently have we been able to systematically examine the relationship between you and your children, Mrs. Jones and the children that she works with, and all environments in which people learn. By testing our hypotheses one at a time, sometimes in a laboratory setting, and sometimes in a natural environment, we have been able to develop a set of general rules that apply to all learning regardless of environment.

Previous to the development of this system, psychologists, educators and others have examined the area of learning and developed many theories about how learning occurs. Oftentimes these theories put the reason for lack of learning inside the child or attribute it so some event long ago that is presently preventing learning from occurring and connot be resolved until those conditions have been eliminated. Our approach takes a rather different point of view and suggests that we can have little control over those things that are now history. We can have a great deal of influence on tomorrow's behavior as a result of the person's interaction with his environment today. It is this dynamic interaction between the person and his environment with which these procedures are concerned.

No person operates in a vacuum; the way he behaves has an effect on the environment in which he exists and that environment in turn has an effect on him. When we speak to someone on the street we have a definite effect on their behavior, and whether or not they answer us has a definite effect on our behavior. It is very difficult to operate in a two person situation without being affected by that interaction.

As you may be able to see by now, we are suggesting that the environment has a great deal of influence over the way a person behaves. When we are talking about teaching children, the major portion of the environment is us—the teachers or parents. Therefore it is our responsibility, if we wish to change somebody else's behavior, to examine very closely the way in which we interact with that person.

The system that we use for describing a learning situation is diagrammed below. By looking at the diagram you can see that it has three major component parts. First, and most important, is the part in the middle which is labeled *behavior*. This is the behavior of the person that we are concerned about or hoping to change. There are many other labels that are used to describe this area as you can see listed below. It is our opinion that what happens to this behavior is a function of those things on either side of that behavior. On the left hand side are those things which occur immediately preceding the behavior. In this particular book we have decided to call those events *cues*.

Cues	*Behavior*	*Consequences*
Signs	Responses	Feedback
Signals	Actions	Reinforcement
Instructions	(Anything	Punishment
The Material	that you do)	(The result of
(Tells you		your behavior)
what is		
expected)		

Cues are those things or the events which set the occasion for that behavior to occur. A good example would be a ringing telephone which would certainly be a cue for us to emit the behavior of picking up the phone. There are many other things in our environment which operate as cues or signs, or signals that tell us when or when not to behave. When a person is not adequately responding to these cues, his behavior is usually looked at as being abnormal. When we do not stop at red lights and go on green lights, we are immediately noticed as being quite different or at least identified as having a problem in that area. When people are not adequately responding to the cues of their environment, we feel that some intervention must take place and they must be taught to respond to those cues.

All of the cues that you respond to in your environment have been learned. You know when to accelerate or decelerate your car, when to enter the restroom reading either men or women, how to respond to a person whether he's giving you a statement or asking you a question, and many other situations which require that you act a specific way depending upon what was presented to you. We feel that these are definitely learned behaviors and when they are not occurring for a child to our satisfaction, then it is indicated to us that we should undertake procedures to teach them what these cues mean.

On the other side of the behavior column there is a whole list of things which we have called consequences. These are the events which occur in our environment as a *result* of our behavior. If you will look at your behavior closely, you will find that it is very difficult for you to behave in any manner that does not result in some type of consequence. In this book we have mainly referred to those consequences as reinforcements. This simply means that the environment has told us whether our behavior should be continued or not. We have either been reinforced or not reinforced for particular behaviors.

If we continually picked up the telephone with no answer

at the other end (we were not reinforced) it would soon have an effect on answering the telephone. However, on the other hand, as exists in most of our cases, when the phone rings and we pick it up, there is usually someone on the other end (Rein-

"HELLO"

forcement). This also has a certain effect on our answering a ringing telephone. The reinforcement that we talk about can basically be thought of as feedback from our environment as to whether or not we should continue our behavior. When these consequences or reinforcements in our environment are providing us with a sufficient amount of information and we are learning from results of our behavior how to behave, we are probably learning at a normal rate. The children who are responding in this way are not the ones about whom we are concerned in this book.

Those children for which obvious consequences are occurring as a result of their behavior and yet who seem not to learn in spite of these consequences are said to have a learning problem. When this sort of thing does occur, it suggests to us, as part of the environment, that we are having very little effect on this person's behavior and we should begin to examine the type of consequences or reinforcement that we are using.

This immediately leads us to another area. We have suggested to you that as a teacher or parent you are a large part

"HELLO, NANCY?"

of the environment. If, in fact, a child is having difficulty learning in this specific environment in which you are involved, it is our position that you are using ineffective cues or reinforcement. The fault for the child's failure to learn, therefore, is yours and not his.

This raises another question. How do we know when what

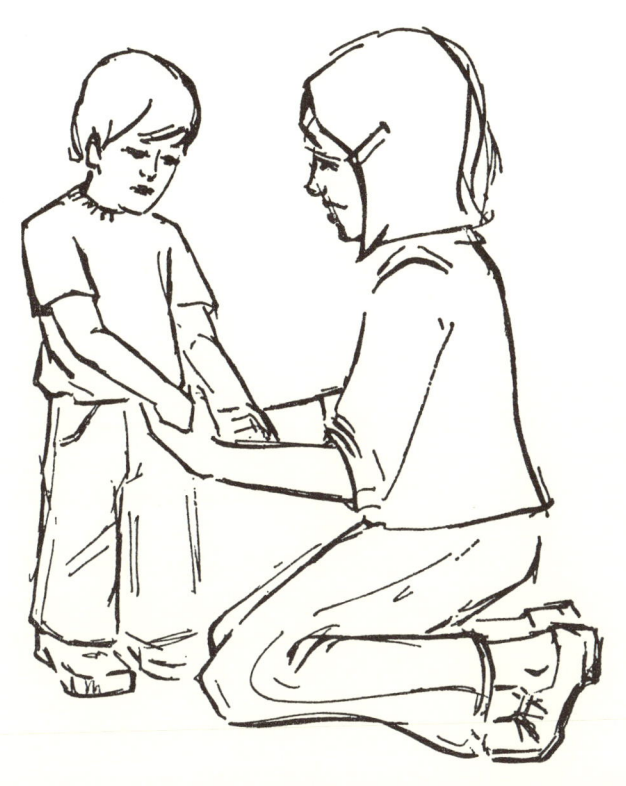

we are doing is not creating the kinds of learning or behavioral change that we would like to see? In some instances this lack of learning is very obvious and can be seen by anybody. However, for the most part we would like to suggest to you that whether or not the cues you are presenting and the types of feedback or reinforcement that you are giving the child is effective is oftentimes a very difficult thing to observe. Oftentimes changes are occurring so slowly that you may not see them occur at all. If you are engaging in behaviors that are not producing any change at all, then we suggest to you to change your strategy. How you make this decision to change your strategy and try something different should not be left up to an occasional observation of the child's behavior or reliance on your memory to supply you with information about the child's performance. This decision should be made based on systematic and accurate observations and recordings of the child's performance. You are all very well aware of the situation which exists when you see your brother's children after you have not seen them for about four years and they look to you as if they have changed enormously, while the parents of those children will suggest to you that they have seen relatively little change in the past few years. If your brother and his wife had made the systematic, frequent and unbiased observations that we are recommending as part of the teaching process, they too would have been aware of the vast changes which had occurred in their children.

We would like to sum up this section by saying that we are going to present to you a model for analyzing and examining human behavior that will put the burden for change on you, the environment. We do not want to put ourselves in a position of making you feel guilty for not being able to achieve the change that you wish. However, the alternative of this is likewise unacceptable—to allow you to arrive at the conclusion that the difficulty lies in the child and therefore there is nothing you can do about it. We are going to suggest strategies and techniques for examining the cues and reinforcements in a given environment and what sort of alterations you might make in both of those areas that will make you more effective as a modifier of behavior. It is our hope that you will be able to see the utility of this approach to help you understand the relationship of behavior to its environment for all persons, including yourself.

Chapter 2

BEHAVIOR

W<small>E ARE GOING</small> to ask you to learn three key words—CUE—REINFORCEMENT—BEHAVIOR, because in teaching your child these are the three things that you will need to understand.

This chapter will talk about BEHAVIOR.

Behavior is a movement, an action; it is anything a person who is alive can do. Behaviors come in all sizes and shapes; there are big BEHAVIORS; there are small behaviors; there are simple behaviors; and there are complex BEHAVIORS. All of these are either BEHAVIORS or behaviors: putting on make-up (BEHAVIOR), pointing a finger (behavior), winking an eye (behavior), driving a car (BEHAVIOR). In other words, everything we do is some type of behavior. A BEHAVIOR, therefore, is considered as a series of actions or movements which may contain many smaller behaviors.

Before you can teach your child, you must decide what behavior you are going to teach him. We call this pinpointing a behavior. In other words, if you tell me that you want to teach the alphabet to your child, I do not really understand what you want to do. Do you want him to learn to read the alphabet, recite the alphabet or write the alphabet? In other words, you will have to be more specific—you will have to pinpoint the behavior. If you tell me that you wish the child to write the alphabet, I should probably suggest to you that you tell me what you want him to do *now* or do first. You could pinpoint the behavior even further by specifying that the child learn to write a particular letter, one at a time.

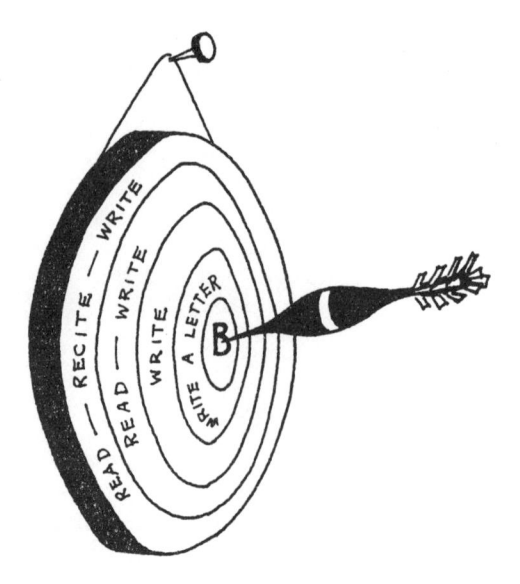

Pinpointing behavior is sometimes quite difficult but it can be simplified if you first learn to *analyze* behavior. When the word "analyze" is used there is usually conjured up in one's mind a vision of men in white coats performing mysterious rites with test tubes, others in shirt sleeves pondering long rows of computer statistics, while still others peer endlessly into microscopes. I think we all agree that this type of analysis is well beyond most of our capabilities. Therefore, when we say you must analyze behavior, we are not asking you to do anything so complex as delving into test tubes, statistics or microscopes. However, we do want you to be able to break BEHAVIOR down into its component parts. In other words, you must examine the BEHAVIOR that you are trying to teach and determine what are all the smaller behaviors that make up that large BEHAVIOR. Remember, we did not expect the child to recognize all the letters of the alphabet at first. Instead, we taught him to recognize one letter at a time.

Perhaps it is best to examine the analysis of BEHAVIORS by using an example. Take the simple (or what appears to be simple) BEHAVIOR of buttering a piece of bread. This is a

BEHAVIOR with which most housewives have extensive experience. Even we husbands are familiar with the process. Let us break this BEHAVIOR down into its component parts; in other words, let us analyze it.

Imagine that the piece of bread, and the removal of the butter from the refrigerator, and lifting the knife from the drawer constitute three different BEHAVIORS; although we must admit that one could not begin to butter the bread without either having first performed those three BEHAVIORS or having them performed for us. As you shall see later, we shall call this relationship of behaviors a chain of behaviors.

Here is how the BEHAVIOR of buttering the bread might be analyzed:

1. Assuming you are right-handed, place your fingers around the knife with your forefinger extended on top of the knife.

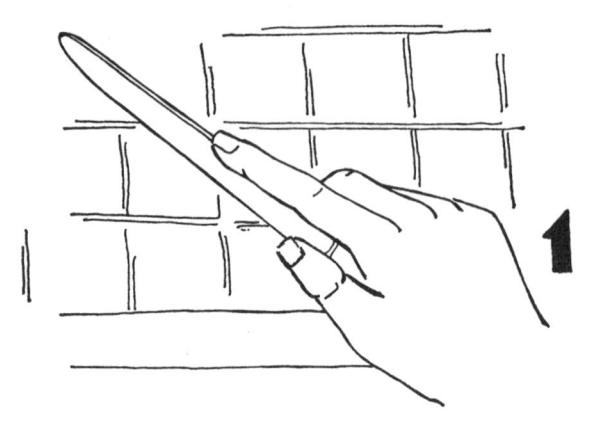

2. Lift the knife from the counter and move it in the direction of the butter dish.

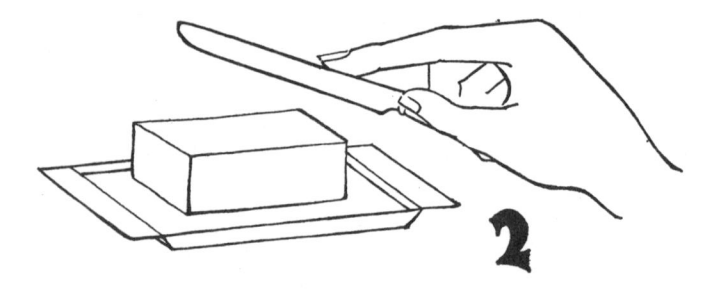

3. Assuming you have a one-quarter pound block of butter, place the blade of the knife approximately one-quarter of an inch from the square edge of the block, resting on top of the block of butter.

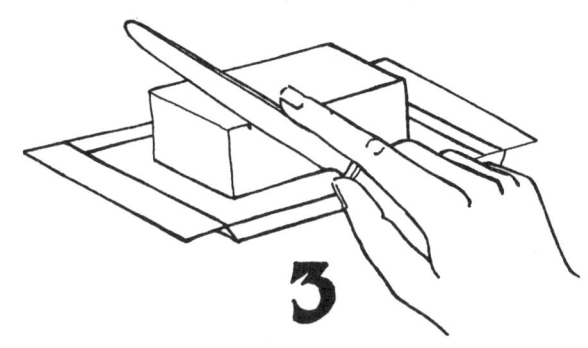

4. Press down with the forefinger causing the knife to cut through the block of butter.

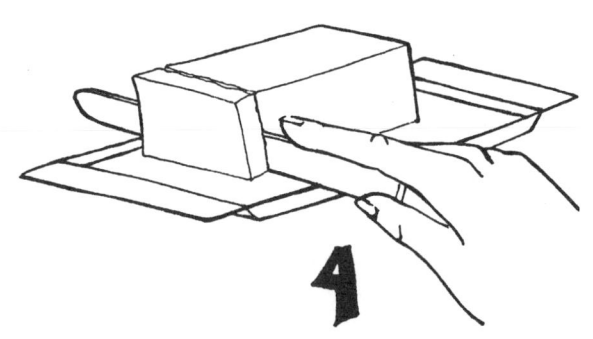

5. Move the knife slightly to the left lifting the cut pat of butter on the knife blade.

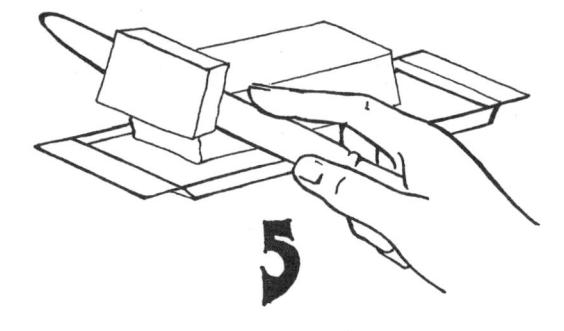

6. Balance the pat of butter on the knife blade; move the knife to the piece of bread.

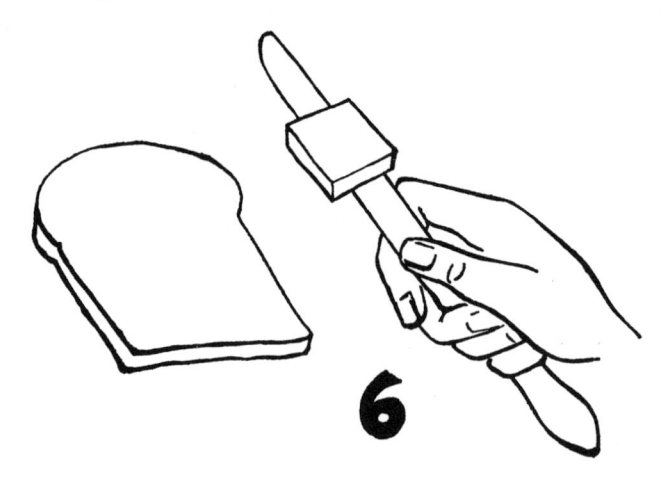

7. Pick the piece of bread up with your left hand, letting it rest in the palm of your hand, being steadied by your fingers.

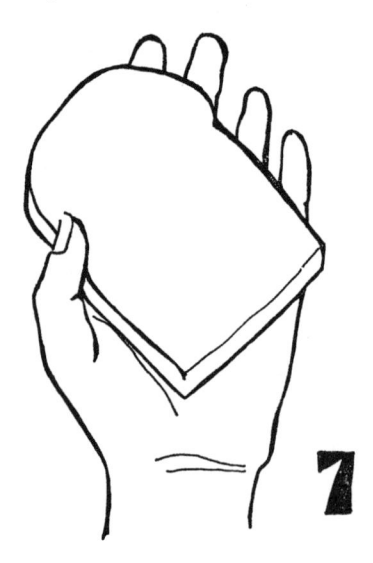

8. Place the pat of butter on the right edge of the bread.

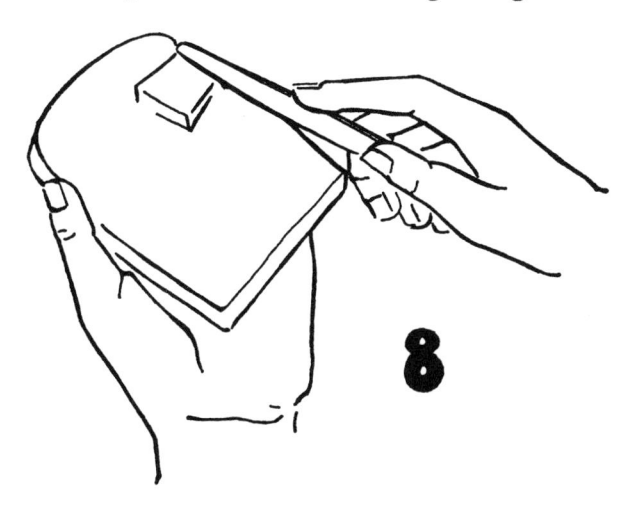

9. Move the knife to the left, pressing the butter on to the bread.

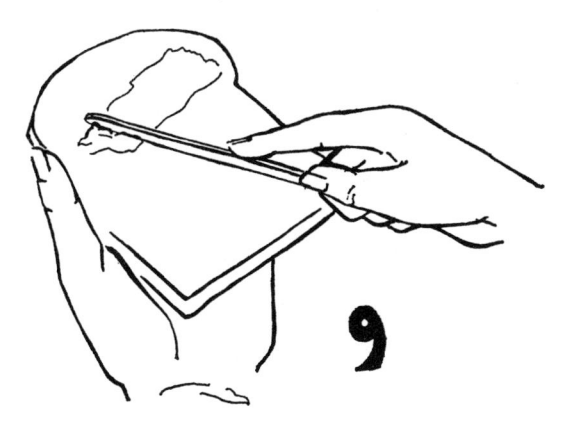

10. Return the knife to the far edge of the bread, adjacent to the position in step 8.

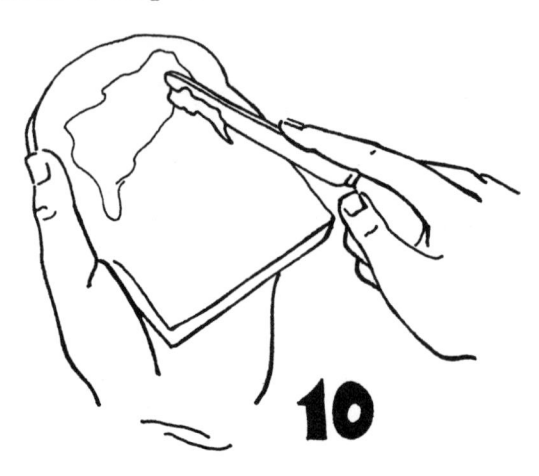

11. Repeat steps 9 and 10 as many times as necessary to continue until the bread is covered with butter.

12. Replace the bread on board.

13. Move knife to butter plate.

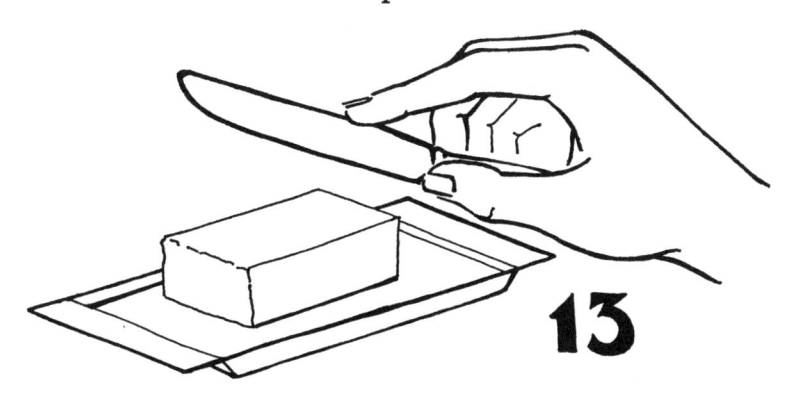

14. Place knife on butter plate.

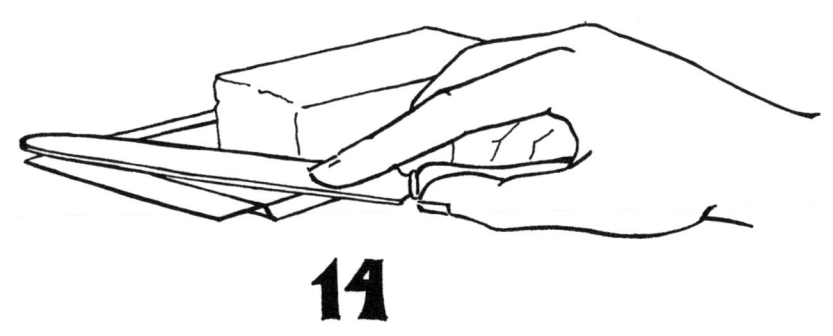

That is how a piece of bread might be buttered. It is a routine activity in which most women and many men engage every day. It is usually not considered difficult, and yet we have broken it down into at least fourteen different smaller behaviors. This indicates a complex or big BEHAVIOR. It requires the use of your two hands. It requires rather fine motor coordination between your eye movements and your hand movements. It requires a sense of judgment which comes about only through experience in that you must determine how much butter you will need to cover the bread. It requires a sense of touch arrived at through experience which tells one how hard to press the butter to make it spread smoothly on the bread.

The point of all this discussion is to emphasize to you that most of the BEHAVIORS which we as adults consider simple and routine are really complex combinations of many smaller behaviors which combine the use of senses, thoughts and motor abilities.

A person's life is filled with such routine BEHAVIORS, complex combinations of manipulation and coordination. Look around you! Examine the small behaviors in pouring a glass of milk, dusting a table, pushing a lawn mower, or two of the most recurring of all—applying make-up and shaving. One of the authors counted the number of small behaviors in his wife's application of make-up in the morning. There were over 200, and this with a woman who is not noted for using much make-up. (Perhaps if you wives tell your husbands the number of steps it takes to apply make-up, they will begin to understand why it takes so long for a woman to get dressed to go out in the evening.) Of course, if we count the number of small behaviors in the BEHAVIOR of shaving, we may find that it should take a man as long to shave as it does for a woman to apply make-up.

But our purpose here is not to talk about your behaviors except to use them to demonstrate to you the complexity of what most people consider simple little tasks. These tasks are usually neither simple nor little, and to the handicapped child they are as complex as the number of steps we are breaking them into. Thus, when we teach a child to butter a piece of bread, to tie his shoe, or to eat his cereal, we have found that the best way to teach this child is to analyze the behavior and break it into small parts and teach each of these parts separately.

But before we turn our attention to teaching your child, you really should try to analyze a BEHAVIOR. Remember that you must look at the big BEHAVIOR and list as a separate little behavior each change in position of any member of the body, whether it be hands or arms, eyes or head, foot or leg, which goes to make up the big BEHAVIOR.

Behavior

Take from out of the closet a shoe that contains a shoelace and analyze the BEHAVIOR of tying a bow in a shoelace.

When you have tried this, turn the page for a pictorial representation of the small behaviors in the BEHAVIOR of tying a shoe.

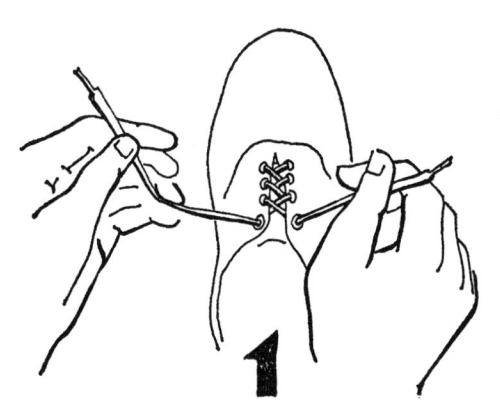

1 Pick up the strings.

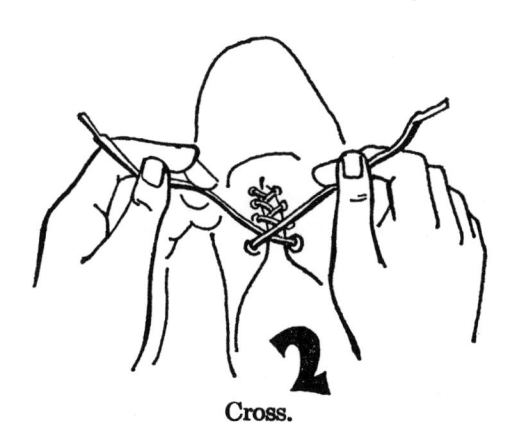

2 Cross.

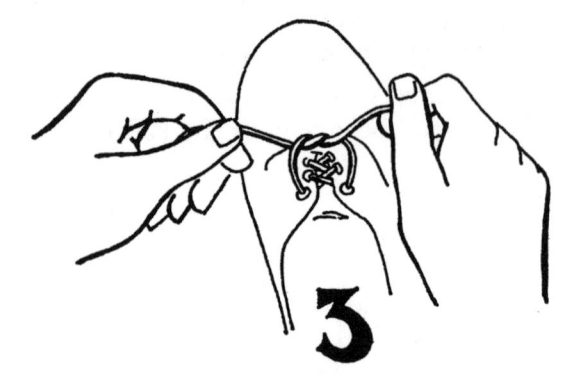

Isn't It Time He Outgrew This?

3 Through.

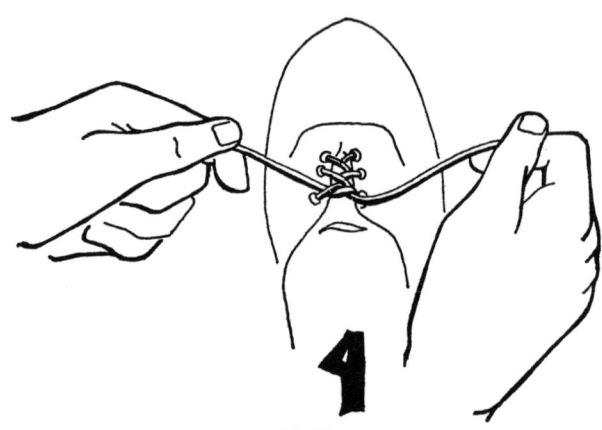

4 Pull.

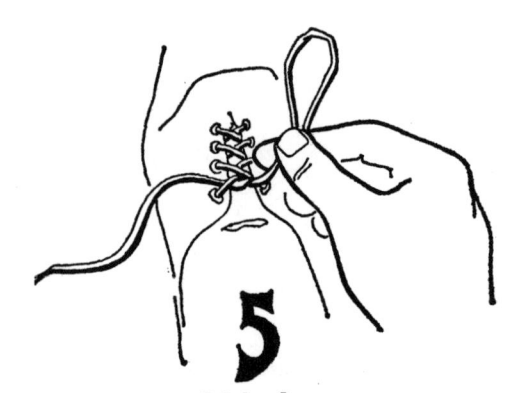

5 Make loop.

Behavior 23

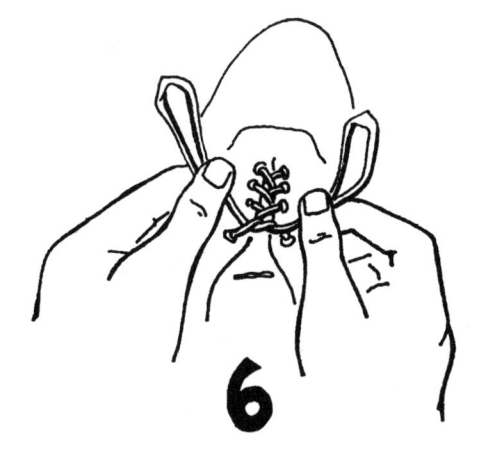

6

Other loop.

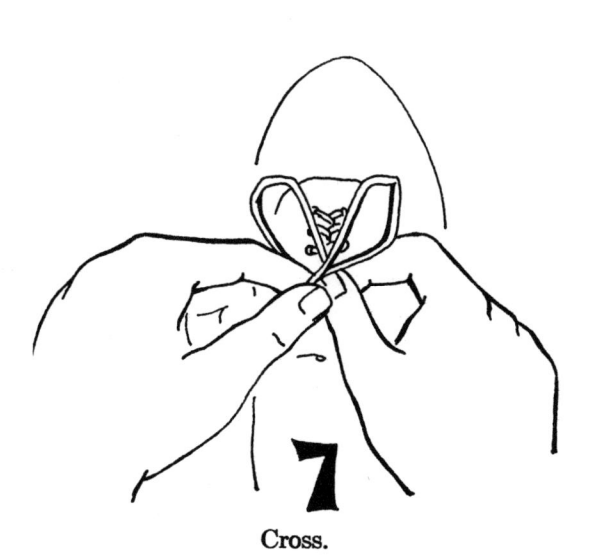

7

Cross.

24   *Isn't It Time He Outgrew This?*

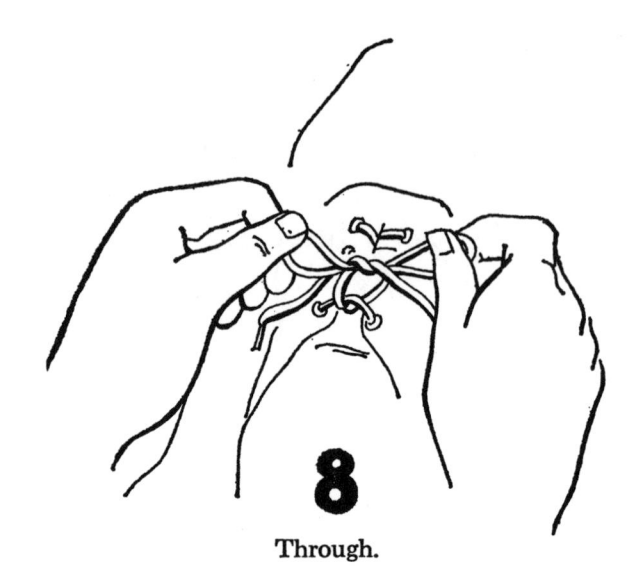

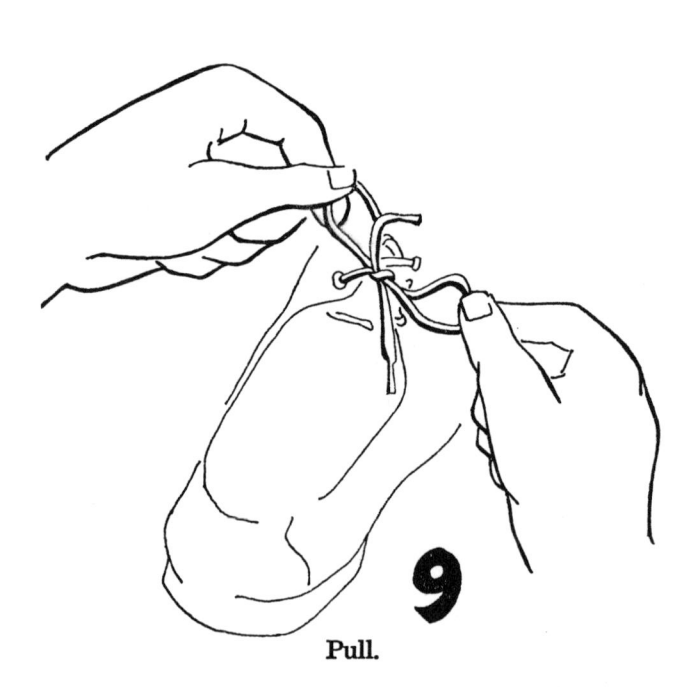

8
Through.

9
Pull.

You now know what behavior is and you now realize that BEHAVIORS can be analyzed or subdivided into smaller behaviors.

We teach handicapped children by teaching them these smaller behaviors one at a time and chaining them together so that they combine to the large BEHAVIOR we are trying to teach.

The first step in teaching the handicapped child is to pinpoint the behavior we wish to teach. Let us once again use the example of buttering a piece of bread. This is a pinpointed behavior. We know exactly what it is that needs to be taught.

The next step is to analyze the BEHAVIOR, that is, break it down into its smaller behaviors.

We are then ready to teach the retarded child the first small behavior, which in the case of the buttering of the bread is that small behavior depicted in Figure 1. We teach him how to hold the knife until we are satisfied that he has demonstrated that he can do that. We then combine the first small behavior with the second small behavior and we teach them together. Thus we have *chained* the behaviors together.

BUTTERING BREAD

All children really learn this way (so do adults). With normal children and adults there is not always the need to break down each BEHAVIOR into component parts and consciously teach each of them separately. However, if you observe a classroom teacher you may be surprised at how often she will break down a learning task into parts.

This learning process is used by most children and adults. The poem is memorized line by line. The processes of a long division problem are learned one after the other. The biology student learns the anatomy of a frog by concentration on one section of the frog's body at a time. The apprentice mechanic learns his trade by tracing the functioning of the automobile's motor, step by gaseous step; and so it is with most learning tasks.

With retarded children learning occurs the same way. The retarded child learns one step, stage or part at a time. The main difference between the retarded child and other children is that it may take longer for the retarded child to learn each part. Moreover, the degree to which each BEHAVIOR must be broken down will depend on the degree of retardation of the child. Some handicapped children will not need the BEHAVIOR broken into very small parts. For instance in tying of shoes, the behaviors described in steps 3 and 4 might be combined into one behavior for some less handicapped children. However, you can almost be sure that if your child is having difficulty learning a behavior, one of the causes of that difficulty may be that you are trying to teach him too much at one time. To achieve success the behavior may have to be broken into finer component parts and these parts chained together.

The examples we have shown you up to this point have chained these behaviors together in only one way—in the order in which they normally occur—or what might be termed a forward chain. We have found that most activities that require motor skills—such as tying a shoe lace, putting on or taking off clothes, riding a bicycle, writing a letter—are better learned by chaining the parts backwards—or learning the last step first. We call this "reverse chaining."

Let us use the example of shoe-tying that we have already illustrated. Step 10 shows the completed task, step 9 shows the child pulling the two loops to tighten the bow. This is the step which we should teach first. We would lead the child through the first eight steps, guiding his hands with ours. When we reached step 9, we would let go of his hands and tell him, "Pull, Johnny!" Initially, we might have to guide his hands after we said, "Pull, Johnny!," but eventually he would do it himself. Then, we would guide his hands through the first seven steps, guiding his hands with ours. When we reached step 8, the placing of one loop under the other, we would have the child do that himself with the command, "Loop under, Johnny!." He would then do steps 8 and 9 by himself. We would then teach step 7 in the same way and so on back through the chain until he was able to perform all the steps by himself and thus accomplish the complex BEHAVIOR of tying his own shoe.

There you are! You now know what a BEHAVIOR and a behavior is. Hopefully, you have now learned to look at BEHAVIOR more critically so that you can analyze it and divide it into smaller behaviors. You have seen small behaviors chained together—both forward and reverse—to form a large or complex BEHAVIOR. You are now ready to learn about cues and reinforcements.

Chapter 3

CUES

THIS CHAPTER IS ABOUT a part of the basic learning process we have been studying. It is the part that we call cues. By cues, we mean all the various signals and directions that tell us what to do, when, where and sometimes how to do it.

It is necessary to have cues if learning is to occur. Cues are a basic part of the learning process. A cue usually precedes a behavior. That behavior is then followed by a reinforcement. For example, to a coke drinker the sight of a soft drink machine serves as a cue for the behavior of pulling a coin out of the pocket and inserting it into the machine and pulling the handle. These series of behaviors are then reinforced by the appearance of the soft drink. Even that simple behavior, however, involves many smaller behaviors with many other cues. We also pick out the button indicating the correct brand of soft drinks. We don't push the button of the machine until we have heard the coin drop all the way down. So all in all, what seemed like a large, smooth BEHAVIOR breaks down to a series of very small cues and very small behaviors.

There are many other kinds of cues with which we come in contact every day. Stop lights are artificial cues whose meaning is agreed upon by everyone. Words are often cues: "Turn on the light"; "Change the channel." We use these to communicate or to direct the behavior of other people. We all agree as to the meaning of the words.

Other kinds of cues do not have meanings which are agreed upon by everyone. These are often personal cues. For example: At a neighborhood party, your wife's slight raising of her eyebrow means, "You've told that joke 27 times before, and if you don't knock it off and get that lampshade off your head, you're really going to get it when you get home!"

People often give personal cues to themselves. If someone else has told us how to get to a particular location, we may repeat those instructions to ourselves as we proceed along the way. Often other kinds of personal cues guide our behavior, even though we may not pay any particular attention to them. A very complex behavior like driving a car involves a variety of cues. Many are quite obvious, like stop lights. Other cues are not so obvious. When driving a car, we hardly pay attention to the cues that are guiding our behavior, such as "the feel of the road," the pressure on our wrists when we have turned the steering wheel far enough, which tells us to release the wheel; the pressure from the brake on our foot, which tells us when we have pushed it far enough. Very likely, when we were first learning to drive a car, someone told us how to do even those very small behaviors. Later we might have told ourselves how to do them and spoken to ourselves as we turned the wheel or pressed the brake. Now all of these behaviors are blended into one smooth BEHAVIOR. The kind of cues that guide our behavior may change as we come to learn that particular behavior better.

Cues, particularly verbal cues, or words, are extremely important when one person is teaching another. We would think, then, that we should use cues very precisely when we are trying to teach another adult. It has been our observation, however, that this is not usually true.

The following conversation actually took place between two people, both well-trained in the principles we hope to show you. One (D) was explaining to the other (J) how to operate a camera. The conversation was as follows:

J. "How do you change the what-da-ya-call it?"
D. "You turn the thing in front."
J. "How far do you wind the beast anyhow?" "What's all that garbage up there?"
D. "You go . . . uh . . . turn this . . ." "When you got plenty of good light and stuff, you get good resolution."
J. "How are these correlated in relation to the gadgets down there?"
. . . and so on.

Surprisingly, J. did learn to use the camera quite effectively. This example does illustrate that the kinds of cues we adults use to communicate with one another are not very precise. Certain kinds of cues that we will call "ADULT CUES" are much different than the kinds of cues that we will give to children. Adults can use words to communicate because we all agree upon the meaning of a word, much like we agree upon the meaning of a stop light. As adults, we have all had many common types of experiences so that when one of us uses a word or refers to an event, the others understand it. Adults' cues are those that contain or assume previous information. Very often, the cues don't make sense literally. For example:

"Keep a stiff upper lip."
"Don't fly off the handle."
"Keep your cool."

It must be obvious that these cues and directions are not meant to be followed literally. However, as adults, we agree upon what they mean figuratively. A very frequent problem in training children is that we use ADULT CUES to teach children. We often use the following cues in an attempt to get children to cease certain undesirable behaviors:

"Knock it off."
"Cut it out."
"Shape up."

or that famous conversation:

> Mother: "What are you doing?"
> Child: "Nothing."
> Mother: "Well, stop it."

When we use *ADULT CUES* with children, we are assuming they have the same information or have had the same experiences as we adults. Of course, this is rarely true. It is quite important that if we are going to be teaching children, that we learn to use *children's cues* rather than adult cues. This is particularly important because we will be dealing with small behaviors rather than large BEHAVIORS. We use *ADULT CUES* for large *BEHAVIORS*. These really cannot be used with children. So we will have to use *children's cues* for small *behaviors*.

Case 1

Ronnie, a deaf child, was seven when we first started working with him. His mother had asked for our help because he was having extreme difficulty in learning the alphabet.

On our first visit we watched Ronnie work on his lessons. His lesson looked like this:

B   X F G B A

Ronnie's job was to find the symbol among the five on the right that matched the letter on the left.

First we wondered if the behavior expected of him was too complex, but in reviewing his past work we felt he should be able to handle the task.

Next, we questioned whether the problem was the reinforcement. But watching his mother told us that she was doing well in reinforcing him.

That left the *cue* to investigate and that's what we found to be the cause of the problem. The cues for correct behavior should be only the various symbols. But Ronnie had discovered other cues. He would slowly move his pencil along the symbols, all the while carefully watching his mother's face. Mother, of course, was looking to see what symbol Ronnie would circle.

Ronnie watched her face until he saw an eye twitch, or an eye movement his mother accidentally made when Ronnie's pencil touched the correct symbol. As soon as he saw his "cue" he circled that symbol. As a result he was demonstrating the right behavior, but for the wrong reason (or cue).

The solution was simply to have mother stand behind Ronnie and if needed redirect him to the paper if he turned around.

In the behavior analysis you did in Chapter 2, you learned how to break the BEHAVIOR of tying a shoe into the small behaviors. So you know already that if you simply told your child, "Tie your shoes," you would be using an *ADULT CUE* for a large *BEHAVIOR*, instead of a child's cue for a small behavior. For some practice, go back to the analysis that you made of tying a shoe and the corrections you made after seeing our version of shoe tying. Beside each behavior that you listed, write a verbal direction or cue which would tell your child to do that behavior. When you have finished, you may practice with your child; or one of you can pretend you are a child and do *exactly* as the instructions say. If you have done a good job, you will end up with a shoe completely tied. If you made a mistake somewhere and you end up with a finger knotted into the shoelace, see how you can correct that with a more precise cue.

When you have finished, look at the list we have made and see how it compares.

There are really three kinds of cues that can be given in teaching shoe-tying to a child. First, the parent should demonstrate each step by doing it herself. Do only one step at a time, and don't go on until the child has mastered that step.

Second, the parent should stand behind the child; place her hands over the child's and guide them through the step once or twice, repeating the spoken cue at each step.

Next the parent should give spoken cues only to the child. The parent should always use the same cue, usually only a single word, and repeat that word each time the child does that step. Except for the cue and the spoken reinforcement there really does not need to be any other conversation.

If you have tried this with your child, you may find particular steps where it is hard for him to understand the cue. You can get him to follow the directions better by exaggerating the cue, much the way you sometimes have to exaggerate reinforcements. He will pay attention to the cue if you make it, in effect, so big that he cannot help but notice it. For example, instead of telling him to put the lace into the hole, you can also point to the hole. You might also draw colored rings around the hole so that they stick out much brighter on the shoe. All of these help exaggerate the cue so your child is more likely to pay attention to it.

As we teach you to analyze BEHAVIOR into small behaviors, we will teach you more about how to use precise children's cues. You will practice how to make the cue match the behavior the child is to learn. Later, as the child begins to learn these behaviors, you will not need to use such precise cues. Each behavior that he has learned will then serve as a cue for the behavior to follow. This is much like our example of how we learned to drive a car. Now, no one needs to tell us how to shift gears, or to put on the brakes. Nor do we have to tell ourselves how to do these things. Instead, the behavior of driving proceeds smoothly because many small behaviors serve as cues for those that follow. As we begin to build little behaviors into large BEHAVIORS, the kinds of cues the children use to guide their behavior will change. Sticking a shoelace through a hole will be cue for sticking the other lace into the next one. Tying one shoe will be the cue for putting on the second.

Chapter 4

REINFORCEMENT

REINFORCEMENT IS a term with which we are all familiar. When we say "That needs to be reinforced," we generally mean that something needs to be strengthened. When we see something around the house such as a chair that is not very sturdy, we often say that we need to reinforce the legs of the chair. When a new bridge is being built, a contractor usually puts reinforcement in the concrete to give the bridge strength.

Reinforcement from our point of view basically means the same thing. If a child does something that we should like to see him do again, we try to reinforce or strengthen that particular behavior. Our usual approach is to tell him what a big boy he is or what a good job he did, or in some way we try to convey to him that we should like him to remember how to do it again. Building a bridge is similar to building new behaviors in a child. It is rare that we see a prefabricated bridge

BEHAVIOR REINFORCEMENT

that is already put together before it is set in place. A more typical approach is to build a bridge one piece at a time and to use reinforcement at key points to insure strength. Just like the building of a bridge, where and how we use reinforcement in learning is extremely important.

Reinforcement in humans also acts as a sort of feedback system which tells the child whether that behavior should stay or go away. If people or events provide us with reinforcement for what we are doing, we will probably do it again. If they do not reinforce our behavior, then the behavior will become weak and less apt to occur.

Reinforcement is a very important item. It occurs in nearly everything we do in our everyday life. As in the case of BIG BEHAVIORS and little behaviors and ADULT CUES and child cues, we also have ADULT REINFORCEMENTS and child reinforcements.

ADULT REINFORCEMENTS are those natural things in our environment that tell us when our performance is acceptable or not. These ADULT REINFORCEMENTS do not have to follow behavior immediately as we have learned to be patient and no longer need reinforcement following everything we do. For example, only occasionally does our wife or neighbor have to tell us that all that work we have done on our lawn "sure makes the house look nice." This is generally sufficient to keep us engaged in long chains of BEHAVIORS including mowing, clipping, planting and fertilizing. Generally this type of reinforcement or feedback is sufficient to produce the upstanding citizens that we are today.

However, many children do not respond adequately to these ADULT REINFORCEMENTS. For example, for you and me a smile of approval from a friend or a teacher is enough reinforcement to tell us that our last behavior was satisfactory. With the retarded child this is often not a sufficient amount of reinforcement to let him know that his last behavior was desirable. When this situation occurs, we must utilize child reinforcements. When we feel that the natural environment of the ADULT REINFORCEMENTS are not doing a good job, it is usually because they have little meaning to the child or they have been given too late. In other words, we are not strengthening his behavior. We, therefore, must resort to child reinforcements that will strengthen his behavior.

You must take caution in picking the type of reinforcement you are going to use. Always remember that what is reinforcing to you or to your neighbor's children might not be a reinforcement to the child you are teaching. The best way to determine whether or not something is a reinforcement is to examine what effect it is having on his behavior. If the behavior strengthens or occurs more frequently, you have found an effective reinforcement. If the behavior is not strengthened, you are probably not using an adequate reinforcement and should use something else. If possible, this something else should be in the form of a reinforcement of known value. For almost every child, we can think of one thing which he likes or enjoys that is extremely reinforcing to him. In the Peanuts Comic Strip it is very easy to see that a powerful reinforcement for Linus is his blanket. For your child it can be a particular food or toy that you know is among his favorites.

These child reinforcements generally fall into three classes:

1. **Primary reinforcements**—These are things which the child will respond to without any previous training. The best example is some type of food—candy, raisin, cereal, and so forth

which will usually work well as the child probably has a preference for one of them.

2. Secondary reinforcements which are of two types—social and tangible. (a) Social—These are the smiles, words of praise, gestures, hugs, and so forth that you use to show your happiness or approval for something your child does. Although these are reinforcing to us as adults, we did not learn to value them immediately when we were children the way we did food. Therefore, they can be called ADULT REINFORCEMENTS in that they are always reinforcing to adults but not always to children. Child reinforcements are very similar to children's cues. They often need to be exaggerated. How does one exaggerate social reinforcement? When a child demonstrates a behavior that you want to strengthen, instead of just saying, "That's a good girl, Mary," you might also clap your hands

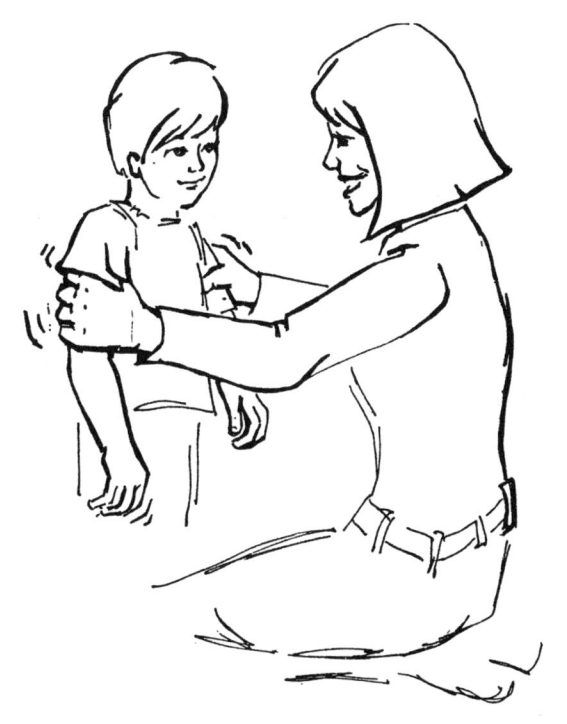

and hug her. In other words, *exaggerated* approval or praise is CHILD REINFORCEMENT. (b) Tangible—These are the things other than food which can be given for reinforcement. They include a wide variety of such things as rides on a rocking horse, watching TV, playing ball, reading a book, music, ringing bells, flashing lights and a thousand other things that can be included under the heading of secondary tangible reinforcements.

3. Generalized reinforcements—Generalized reinforcements consist of those things which can be used to obtain other reinforcements. An example might help to clarify; a generalized reinforcement could be gold stars, marks, grades, allowance, etc. After the child gets so many of these, a system is set up where he can trade them for other reinforcements of his choice. You and I work for these kind of reinforcements and we call them money or trading stamps.

There are some general rules of thumb you should always follow when applying child reinforcements. First, it makes no sense to give candies, tokens or goodies if you do not at the same time give a natural reinforcement and/or ADULT REINFORCEMENT, such as attention, approval and praise. After all, our goal is to make ADULT REINFORCEMENT powerful and we do so by pairing it with a known child reinforcement such as orange juice which we already know is very powerful with a particular child. You will get an effect in reverse similar to "guilt by association," where the noneffective ADULT REINFORCEMENT becomes more powerful by being associated with something the child likes.

Another important thing to remember is that no matter what type of reinforcement you are giving, regardless of the situation, you should always give it immediately following the child's behavior that you wish to strengthen. If a child demonstrates a desirable behavior that you would like continued or repeated, then you must reinforce it quickly. The longer you wait, the less effective your reinforcement will be.

When building a bridge, we have to use enormous supports until the cement dries. The same is true with children. We

BEHAVIOR-REINFORCEMENT
BEHAVIOR ——————— REINFORCEMENT

often have to use exaggerated or child reinforcement until the more natural or ADULT REINFORCEMENTS can work by themselves. Sooner or later we shall have to take the exaggerated support out of our system for we cannot leave the scaffold on the bridge nor can we leave the child in the condition where he is dependent upon rewards and goodies for everything he does. We have used these exaggerated reinforcements to get behavior started and to become stable. Once this is accomplished, we must pull these exaggerated reinforcements out of the system. If we pull them out too fast, the behavior and the bridge will both lose strength. Children have many more complex qualities than bridges have, so as we begin to withdraw the exaggerated reinforcement from a particular behavior, because it is becoming stable, we can now use the exaggerated reinforcement on a new behavior which we wish to strengthen. We call this withdrawal of the exaggerated reinforcement "fading." In other words, once we get the behavior going, we use only the ADULT REINFORCEMENTS occasionally and we try to let the child develop self-satisfaction out of the job he has now learned to do. We save our child's reinforcements for other new behaviors that we decide to teach the child.

An example may illustrate this last point and how fading works: One of our authors, who was conducting many classes with parents, was met one evening upon returning home by his wife holding the hand of his two-year-old son.

"This is your son," she said, "he is not toilet trained. You teach all these parents how to toilet train their children. How about toilet training your own?"

Our hero, whose alias for this story will be SAM, knowing that his professional reputation was at stake, valiantly approached the task under the critical eye and tongue of his wife. Following the procedures prescribed in our toilet training chapter, Sam first determined when Junior was most likely to "go potty." He then sat him on the potty at that time.

Sam waited patiently by the door for the tell tale sound of the urine hitting the potty. At last it came—and with it Sam delivered the reinforcement which he felt Junior would most appreciate.

First, he let out a cheerful, "That-a-boy, Junior" (social reinforcement, exaggerated); then he flashed the bathroom lights on and off rapidly (tangible reinforcement); and finally, because both Sam and his son are part Indian, Sam performed an old tribal war dance with appropriate war whoops. Junior loved it! This ritual was repeated, each time Junior went to the potty as he was supposed to.

Time passed with an increasing number of successes and Junior began to tell Dad that he had to go potty. Sam realized that it was time to begin the fading process. The first thing Sam pulled out of the system was the flashing bathroom lights. The exuberant "That-a-boy, Junior" and the Indian War Dance remained. Gradually, however, the war dance became shorter and less intense, and before long it was only one war whoop. Then the social praise became less enthusiastic, and Sam began to position himself away from the bathroom door where Junior could not see him. Junior then had to say, "I'm done, Dad,"

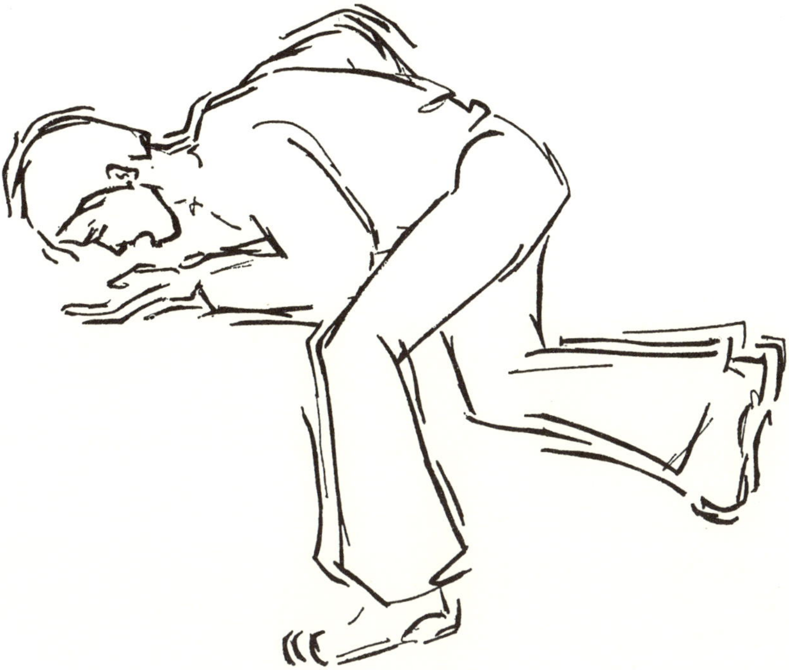

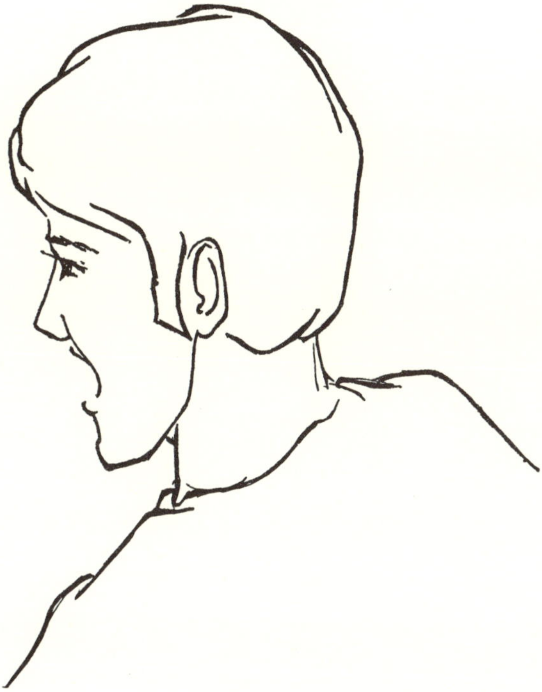

and Sam would reply, "Good." Before long, no longer was the "Good" even necessary. Junior was toilet trained and was going "potty" by himself because he knew it was the thing to do.

Thus, a period of training began with some very exaggerated and child reinforcements. As the child demonstrated he could do the behavior, the child reinforcements were gradually reduced and in their place was established ADULT REINFORCEMENT.

Chapter 5

BEHAVIOR PROBLEMS

Some of the most frequent concerns for parents of mentally retarded children are behavior problems. We cannot say whether the mentally retarded child has more behavior problems or worse behavior problems than do children who are not retarded. We can say, however, that his behavior problems are quite similar to the problems any child may have. For the most part they are rather unfortunate behaviors which have been *learned* as a reaction to environmental situations. They have been learned much the same way all behaviors, both good and bad, have been learned. That is, the behavior problems of the retarded and nonretarded child alike are behaviors developed in response to certain cues, and they are reinforced by their effect upon people or things.

It is often rather easy to see how good behavior is learned. When our child does something that we like, we are happy about it. We tell him we are happy and reinforce him for that behavior. Furthermore, he seems to enjoy the reinforcement and attention he receives. That is why it is often all the more difficult to see what is reinforcing his bad behavior. Sometimes he continues to behave in a way that we do not like even after we have clearly told him that we disapprove of that behavior. He may continue to engage in behavior at which we disapprove even following spankings, being sent to his room or any other thing parents often do to stop unwanted behavior.

To attempt to understand the whys and wherefores of behavior problems, we will have to take a very close look at them.

Let us take a look at a very frequent behavior problem—temper tantrums. Temper tantrums, like any other behavior, follow certain cues. Perhaps temper tantrums follow cues from a parent, such as demands, directions, requests, commands, and so forth. Perhaps because of his past failures in being able to successfully comply with these requests, the child has developed this behavior. These may represent his reaction to a rather unpleasant situation. Furthermore, they may be reinforced in a number of ways. Sometimes the parent, *without meaning to*, supports or reinforces that behavior.

Let us try to clarify the situation by looking at a boy named Billy. Every evening at bedtime when his parents ask Billy to go to bed he throws a temper tantrum. He shouts, screams and kicks his feet. He informs them in his own rather direct way that he refuses to go to bed and wants to watch more TV. Billy's parents attempt to control the behavior in a number of ways. Initially they try to reason with him or to comfort him in an attempt to get him to cease his temper tantrum. Finally, in desperation, they state that if he will stop the temper tantrum and be quiet, he can watch fifteen more minutes of TV before going to bed. Sometimes this is enough to stop the temper tantrum. At other times it only postpones it another 15 minutes. Most of the time, however, Billy will cease the temper tantrum because of the reinforcing effect of the comforting and attention he is receiving from his parents, and because of the additional time he can spend watching TV. Even though he stops the behavior, he has been reinforced for it. And so, the next time a similar request to go to bed is made of him he will throw another temper tantrum.

If we were to analyze Billy's behavior, we might do it in the following simplified way:

CUE	BEHAVIOR	REINFORCEMENT
Demand by parent to go to bed	TEMPER TANTRUMS	Attention from parents and TV

Behavior Problems 49

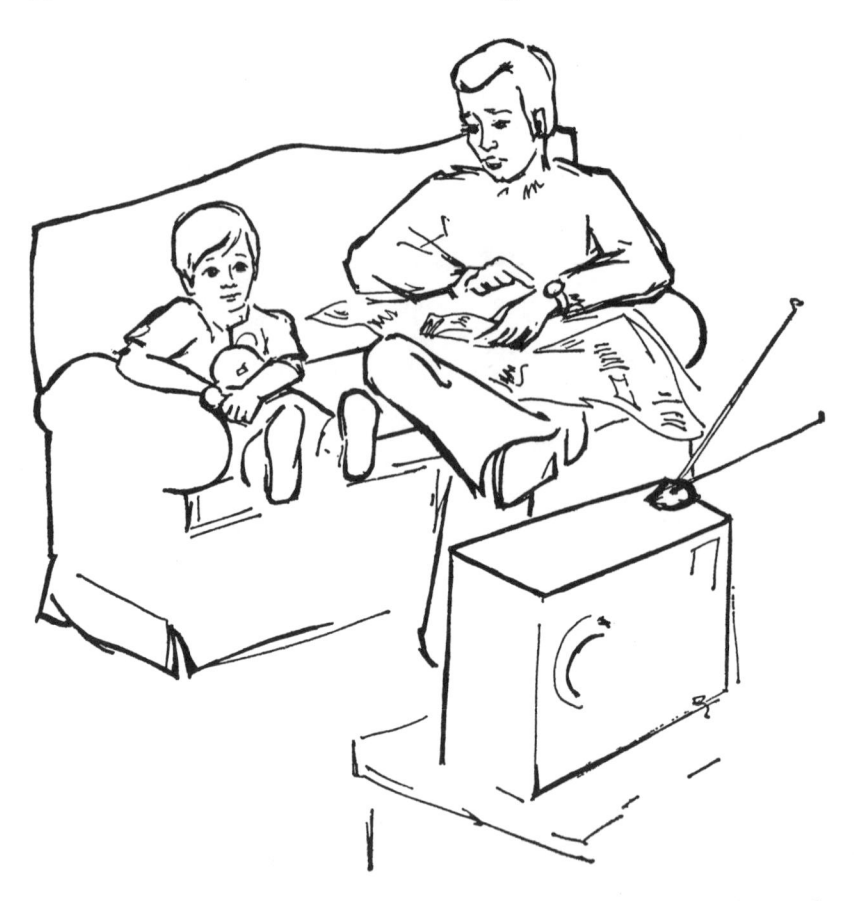

We are saying then, that the temper tantrums follow the cues from the parent to go to bed and are reinforced both by the attention he received from the parent and by the additional time he spends watching TV. There is another important item we must look at. Very often it happens that the parent develops behaviors which eventually quiet the temper tantrum, but behaviors which, nevertheless, make it more likely the tantrum will occur in the future. This is quite important, because in the situation we are describing, Billy's parents are also being reinforced. If the parent can cease the temper tantrum by comforting the child or by allowing him to watch TV, the parent is reinforced by the removal of that unpleasant tantrum. All reinforcements do not have to be something pleasant or enjoyable or good or fattening. Reinforcement can also occur when a behavior results in the removal of something unpleasant. For example, many of us have learned to end unpleasant phone conversations with someone to whom we really do not want to talk by saying, "There's someone at the door now; I'll have to hang up." Those statements are reinforced because they remove us from an unpleasant situation.

Much the same kind of thing is happening with Billy's parents. Looking at their behavior it could be analyzed in the following manner:

CUE	BEHAVIOR	REINFORCEMENT
Billy's temper tantrums	Soothing and comforting Billy and delaying bedtime by allowing him to watch TV	Stopping of temper tantrum and resulting peace and quiet

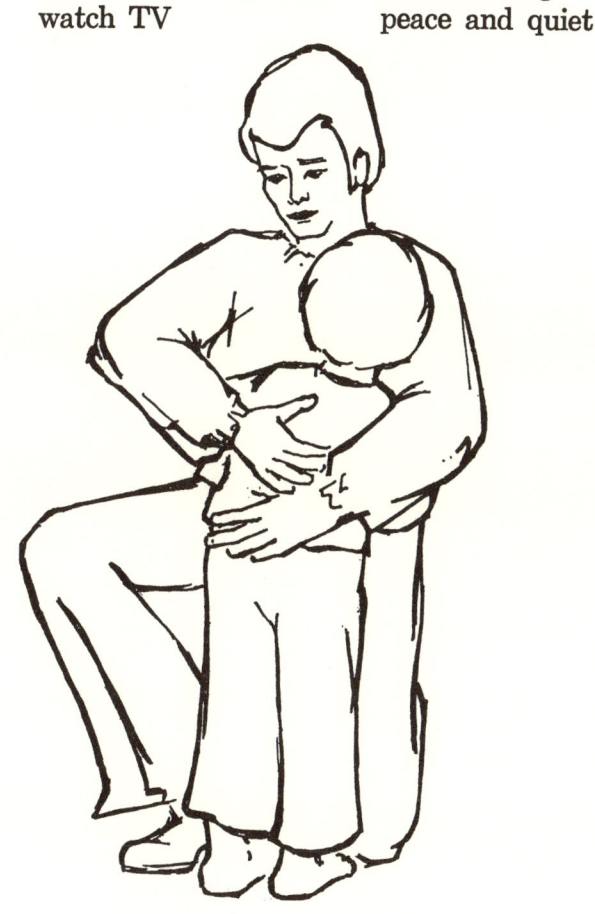

We have found in very many cases that children and parents learn to support and reinforce each other in a way which maintains the behavior problems of the child. The parent is reinforced by the stopping of a temper tantrum; the child is reinforced by the comfort he receives, or by getting his own way.

In many cases the situation is much more complex than is the situation with Billy. We do think, however, that in nearly every case the behavior in question is a behavior that has been *learned*. Therefore, it can be *unlearned*. For nearly every behavior problem we may come across there are two basic procedures for handling it. First, the reinforcement for undesirable behavior must be removed or weakened or diminished. Second, a substitute behavior must be developed to take the place of the undesirable: if you wish to eliminate temper tantrums at bedtime, you must also teach the behavior of going to bed quietly and promptly.

Unfortunately we cannot provide you with any surefire cure-all for all behavior problems. What we can give you in the next few pages, however, are some general directions that you can use to analyze situations that cause behavior problems. This should allow you to devise a program for your child's behavior problem. We will show you some ways in which you can come up with techniques for removing the reinforcements for undesirable behavior and developing other behaviors to replace them. Following this we will give you some practice by quoting you cases of children who have frequent kinds of behavior problems. We will ask you to set up a hypothetical program, and then show you the kind that we might set up. Following that, you should be ready to start your own program. To aid you in this we will give you a general set of questions to ask about your child's behavior. These questions should lead you into coming up with the kind of specific technique that you will need.

We have already discussed some of the ways in which you teach new behaviors. Generally, you do this by presenting reinforcements following the *desired behavior*. In the opposite sense, you eliminate behaviors by *withdrawing* or *removing* the reinforcement following the undesired behavior. This must be followed up by reinforcing a new behavior. At the very least you will have to develop the opposite behavior: you want to eliminate not going to bed and develop going to bed.

There are several things Billy's parents could do to eliminate the reinforcements for temper tantrums. First, they could turn off the television. This would eliminate the possibility that Billy might be watching it while he throws a temper tantrum. It should also help to get the idea across to him that he will not get to watch television by this behavior. Second, the parents could cut off their attention by finding something to do and ignoring Billy until he stopped. They could read a newspaper, discuss the day's activities, debate the merits of the antiballistic missile system or start a quick game of Monopoly®. They should continue ignoring Billy until the temper tantrum stops. When it has stopped for at least a minute, they could go over to Billy and reward him for acting grownup. Billy may very well be ready for bed by now. On the other hand he might start a second temper tantrum. However, if his parents again ignored it, they would notice one very important thing. The second temper tantrum will be shorter than the first one. If they are consistent in ignoring the behavior, they will find that the temper tantrums become increasingly shorter and finally disappear. The real trick is in being consistent and in not giving in to Billy, for as you will see shortly this would produce a much worse tantrum in the future.

The second part of the program involves, of course, the development of other kinds of behaviors to take the place of the temper tantrums. We want Billy to go to bed quietly. So we will have to find a reinforcement for that behavior. We know that Billy enjoys television; in fact that is part of the reinforcement for throwing the temper tantrum. So let's make television the reinforcement for going to bed. You can tell Billy that his bedtime is 7:30, but that he can earn an 8 o'clock bedtime. He earns the later bedtime by his good behavior. He can earn fifteen minutes of TV watching by being good throughout the evening. If he goes to bed quietly and promptly without a temper tantrum at the appointed time, he could earn fifteen more minutes of TV watching the next night. You might give him a chart to write down the fact that he has earned an extra fifteen minutes by going to bed quietly. You might give him a token or a poker chip which could be traded for fifteen minutes of later bedtime. These he would get following an evening of good behavior and the behavior of quietly going to bed at the appointed time. Thus, by ignoring the undesirable behavior and reinforcing the desired behavior with TV, praise, attention, etc., you may be able to completely eliminate the problems at bedtime.

From the example of Billy, we can give you some general rules about eliminating and developing behavior. The first general rule is that you must withdraw, cut off, diminish, eliminate, remove, etc. the reinforcement for undesirable behavior. If you can isolate what is reinforcing a child's bad behavior and arrange the situation so this reinforcement no longer follows it, then you are well on the road to stopping that behavior. At this point, however, we must tell you that there is one thing you can surely expect to see when using this type of approach. When you begin cutting off the reinforcement for bad behavior, you can, almost without exception, expect to see your child try harder and harder for a short period of time to get that reinforcement you are now withholding. The old saying that "It's going to get worse before it gets better," is very true when we begin to withhold reinforcement. This is not an unusual or strange way for a child to behave. As a matter of fact, you behave the same way when you are put into a similar type of situation. Nearly all of us have the behavior of putting money into machines, such as Coke machines, cigarette or candy machines. We have developed the behavior of putting the money in, pulling the handle and being reinforced by the appearance of the Coke, candy, etc. Since this behavior has been reinforced perhaps thousands of times, it is a very strong behavior. Suppose you put a dime in the Coke machine, the same machine you have been going to for many months. But this time you do not get the Coke. Chances are you will not shrug your shoulders, turn and walk away. Of course what you do is to hit the machine, say a few words under your breath, jiggle the handle a few times or do anything else that might get the Coke out of the machine. Your child does much the same thing when you begin to ignore behaviors. He may demonstrate that behavior, initially, much more often or more rapidly than he had in the past.

If the Coke still does not appear, we get more strenuous in our behavior. We pound the machine harder, kick it with our foot, etc. That is, we try other behaviors which, in the past, may have been rewarded by the appearance of a Coke. In the same way your child may try other behaviors besides temper tantrums that he has been rewarded for in the past. Besides temper he might try screaming or jumping, yelling dirty words, hitting his brother, etc.

Suppose, now, after all of your kicking and pounding of the

Coke machine, the Coke comes out. What do you think you will do the next time you go to a Coke machine and the Coke does not come out after you drop the dime and pull the handle? Right. You will kick it and pound it just the way you did before you were reinforced previously. This is also what happens to a child who engages in bad behavior and initially the parents attempt not to give in to it. But finally they cannot endure it any longer and give in to him. The next time he throws a temper tantrum he will be able to go just that much longer and exert that much more effort because he was reinforced for that in the past. This is why it is so crucial to be consistent in withholding the reinforcement and not to give in even though it may be unpleasant temporarily.

There are other techniques for withdrawing reinforcement One of the most important questions you will have to ask is whether you do have control of that reinforcement which you know maintains the undesirable behavior. If the behavior is your attention or the TV, you certainly have control of that. In other cases you may not have control of the reinforcement—his brothers' and sisters' laughter, etc. Or, if the temper tantrum gets out of control and the child begins breaking lamps, you cannot continue to ignore that behavior. Nor can you wait until you have run out of lamps. In both of those cases you may have to do something else than just sit there while the temper tantrum occurs. One technique is, instead of removing the reinforcement from the child, remove the child from the reinforcement. You can take him by the hand, lead him to another room, such as the bedroom and close the door. Leave him there until the temper tantrum stops. Then, when it has stopped for a few minutes, go in and reward him for being quiet.

Now when we say take him to his bedroom and leave him there, there is one other factor that must be considered. When we were younger, being sent to our rooms probably was a very unpleasant situation. This may not be the case for your children. Sending a child to a room these days frequently means putting him in a place where he has a portable TV set, a record player, books, 72 varieties of toys, 13 model airplane kits, three transistor radios and a fifteen foot scale model lunar landing station. In other words, putting him in his room may not remove him from all reinforcement. For that reason it may be better to use a relatively bare room or a bathroom, in other words a room where there is very little which he can use as a reinforcement. In this way you can be successful at cutting off the reinforcement following that behavior.

Now, the other side of the coin is to develop new behaviors to replace the old ones. One of the best ways to eliminate undesirable behaviors and develop new ones is to try to find behaviors that we call *"incompatible."* This means we should try to find a behavior to strengthen that the child cannot do at the same time he does the undesirable behavior. Suppose, for example, we have a six-year-old child who is sucking his

thumb. You might try to get rid of this behavior by reinforcing him for doing something with his hands that makes it impossible for him to get the thumb in his mouth, like playing catch with a ball. While throwing, catching or holding the ball, he cannot suck his thumb.

There is another gimmick which might be helpful to you in terms of thinking up things to do that are incompatible with the unwanted behavior. First, try to think of the most exaggerated thing that you can—something that would absolutely insure that the unwanted behavior could not occur. Think of something exaggerated and ridiculous; then begin to work backwards, thinking of things less exaggerated. For example, let us take the case of the boy who is sucking his thumb. One very ridiculous and exaggerated thing we could do to absolutely insure no thumb sucking would be to have him wear boxing gloves on his hands. Particularly if he is a small boy, the size of the thumbs in the boxing gloves is just too large to get into his mouth. So, of course, this procedure would work. But there might be some unfortunate side effects: for example, his friends might laugh at him because of his silly appearance. Also, while wearing boxing gloves is incompatible with thumb sucking, it is also incompatible with lots of other behaviors. It would be quite difficult for him to do any writing or coloring. He would also have a good deal of trouble in feeding himself, since using silverware requires a good deal of finger dexterity. Other kinds of activities requiring fine muscular control of the hands and fingers would be quite difficult if not impossible. After we begin to notice that his pants are continually wet, we would realize that unzipping one's pants is very difficult when one is wearing boxing gloves. So for all these reasons this is still not too good an idea, and so we would look for one a bit less exaggerated.

We could wrap a huge wad of adhesive tape around his thumb which would make his thumb too large to get into his mouth, but leave the rest of his fingers free. This is not too bad an idea, and it is a little less exaggerated than the previous one. We could let him carry 10 pennies around with him in his hand, and if he goes a specified period of time without opening his hand to suck his thumb and thus dropping the pennies, he will spend his pennies on something he likes. We might let him spend his pennies on activities which are enjoyable, but which also require the use of his hands, like building model airplanes. In this way he would be doing something else incompatible with sucking his thumb.

In our example of Billy we suggested reinforcing behaviors that are incompatible with temper tantrums. That is why we said you should go over and reward him when he has been quiet following a temper tantrum. For Billy cannot be both quiet and throw a temper tantrum simultaneously. Neither can he refuse to go to bed when he is going to bed quietly. So we suggested rewarding that behavior as well. In some situations you will have to wait out the undesirable behavior, then reinforce the desirable.

Now we are going to present you with some short descriptions of further typical behavior problems. We will ask you on the following pages to list what you think was the cue that set off the behavior. Also, try to describe the behavior as clearly as you can from the sketchy information we give you. Then try to indicate what you think is reinforcing that behavior. All the essential information is available in the cases if you can just look closely enough for it. Then list the techniques that you would use to withdraw reinforcement from the undesired behaviors as well. As you finish each one, turn to our answers and see if we are both heading in the same direction.

CASE NUMBER 1

Freddie, 3½, has not yet learned to talk. He does seem to be able to make his wishes known quite easily, however. For example, this Thursday afternoon Freddie's mother, Mrs. Smith, had her neighbor in for coffee. Freddie was watching cartoons on televeision. Suddenly Freddie let out an enormous yell. The coffee cups on the serving tray rattled in their saucers. Two pictures fell off the wall. Freddie had blasted once again! The yell was long and loud, lasting approximately five seconds. Mrs. Smith quickly jumped up and changed the TV channel. Freddie ceased his yelling almost immediately.

The neighbor, after recovering her composure, asked Mrs. Smith, "What makes Freddie do that?

"He does that whenever he wants something changed or would like something to happen right away," she replied.

"Do you enjoy that?" asked her neighbor.

"No. But if we act right away, like changing the channel, he stops his blasting very quickly."

'How long has he been doing this?"

"Well, he started a few weeks ago, and it wasn't too bad then. But he seems to be getting worse. We probably shouldn't give in to him, but he does shut up right away as soon as we do what he'd like. And he really doesn't talk any other way, and I suppose since we've known he's retarded, we try to do whatever we can for him. Maybe it's just a stage he's going through."

Case Number 1—Questions

Question 1: Please describe the behavior you would like to eliminate.
Question 2: What is the cue or situation that sets off the behavior?
Question 3: What do you think is reinforcing this behavior? Remember there may be more than one source of reinforcement maintaining that behavior.
Question 4: Do you think the parent is being reinforced as well? How?
Question 5: How would you remove, cut off, or eliminate the reinforcement that you think is maintaining his behavior?
Question 6: What incompatible behavior would you develop? Try to be specific. Try thinking of the cue it would follow.
Question 7: How could you measure whether you are having any success? Clue: When you pick a measurement, instead of measuring before you try to change the behavior, be sure you measure the behavior you are trying to increase as well as the behavior you are trying to decrease.

Case Number 1—Answers

Answer 1: Loud, long yells.
Answer 2: A. The television playing and Freddie wanting the TV channel to be changed sets off the yells.
B. Apparently from what the mother says any situation that requires verbal communication by Freddie to make his wishes known also sets off yelling.
Answer 3: A. Mother responds and pays attention to the child.

B. Mother complies with what is apparently Freddie's wish.

C. Perhaps getting his own way or watching the television show he wants to.

Answer 4: A. Yes.

B. The mother is being reinforced in that Freddie stops his yelling when she changes the television channel and complies with Freddie's "request."

Answer 5: A. First of all, mother will have to ignore the yelling and simply wait it out.

B. She might also turn off the television as long as he is yelling, and not turn it back on until he is quiet.

Answer 6: The basic incompatible behavior must be some acceptable form of communication other than the "blasting." The mother should therefore establish as acceptable some type of communication Freddie is now capable of, such as a quieter form of the yell, or a few simple words or syllables. She should then require him to make an appropriate request and then she should comply with it. She might also set up many training situations in which Freddie is required to ask for a number of things after which she complies with the requests.

Answer 7: In general, the measurement system should record the frequency of Freddie's blasts or yelling per day or per hour, or for some other reasonable time period. Mother should start a few days before she tries the treatment program, to get some estimate of his level of yelling. She should also record the frequency of the appropriate communications by him that she has decided upon. Next, she should introduce the treatment program discussed above and continue to record the frequency of blasting and frequency of appropriate talking and continue to record this until the end of the program.

CASE NUMBER 2

Same Old Saturday Night

It is Saturday night again. It is the Wilson's only night out during the week, and on this Saturday they are going to dinner and movies. And every Saturday night it is the same old routine with Billy. Maybe he hates baby-sitters; maybe he just doesn't want his parents to leave him. In any event, Saturday night is always accompanied by much screaming, yelling and crying.

Billy, age four, knows the baby-sitter; she sits quite often for him, often on other occasions than Saturday. But whenever the Wilsons leave, Billy starts his temper tantrum. The baby-sitter says they really do get along quite well and after the Wilsons are gone he settles down quite rapidly and even has a good time during the evening. It seems to be the leaving that causes all the trouble.

This Saturday, Mrs. Wilson feeds Billy his dinner and he is quite happy. While the parents are getting dressed, Billy is quietly watching television. When they are all dressed and ready to go, he is still engrossed with TV. Then the baby-sitter arrives; the Wilsons kiss Billy goodby and head out the door. Then it starts. He yells, screams, sits on the floor and kicks his feet. Then he runs to the door and lets out a large bloodcurdling yell. The neighbors open their door. Drivers on the street slam on their brakes.

Mother is outside and now returns to explain to Billy that they are only going away for a little while and they will be back that evening. Billy just yells all the louder. Her explanations are not doing any good and so Mrs. Wilson turns to leave again. She gets outside and halfway to the car. Mr. Wilson is waiting behind the wheel. Billy screams again. Mother returns and tries to comfort him once more.

It is now almost 7 o'clock and their dinner reservations were for 6:30. Mr. Wilson leaves the car and comes to the door. Mrs. Wilson turns around and sympathetically looks at him.

He yells, "No. We're going. Last week was the last time we are going to change our plans and stay home on Saturday night."

They both walk to get into the car once again. Billy is still yelling at the window. Mrs. Wilson turns as if to re-enter the home. Mr. Wilson says, "No," and several other things as well. They both get into the car and leave for an evening they probably will not enjoy and Mrs. Wilson wonders about next Saturday night.

Case Number 2—Questions

Question 1: Please describe the behavior you would like to eliminate.

Question 2: What is the cue or situation that sets off the behavior?

Question 3: What do you think is reinforcing this behavior? Remember there may be more than one source of reinforcement maintaining that behavior.

Question 4: Do you think the parent is being reinforced as well? How?

Question 5: How would you remove, cut off or eliminate the reinforcement that you think is maintaining his behavior?

Question 6: What incompatible behavior would you develop? Try to be specific. Try thinking of the cue it would follow.

Question 7: How could you measure whether you are having any success? Cue: When you pick a measurement, instead of measuring before you try to change the behavior, be sure you measure the behavior you are trying to increase as well as the behavior you are trying to decrease.

Case Number 2—Answers

Answer 1: Screaming, sitting on the floor kicking his feet, letting out yells, etc.

Answer 2: Apparently the cue is the parents' beginning to leave the house on Saturday evening. This usually occurs shortly after the arrival of the baby-sitter.

Answer 3: The attention the mother gives him by going back and talking to the child, kissing him, trying to comfort him, perhaps making promises, etc., seems to reinforce this behavior. Also, the previous Saturday the parents changed their mind and stayed at home with him the entire evening, rather than leave him there with the baby-sitter.

Answer 4: Mother may be reinforced by giving in to the child. This could occur if, when she does leave him to go out for the evening, she worries and is quite anxious about what is happening at home and wondering how he is getting along. Therefore, if she stayed home on Saturday evening and gave in to him, she could alleviate her fears and her anxiety.

Answer 5: The parents will have to leave very quickly without continually going back and attending to him.

Answer 6: The behavior that must be developed is appropriate and quiet goodbyes without temper tantrums or yelling when the parents have to leave the house. This could be developed by setting up a program where a special reward could be earned by him for acting like a "big man" when they leave. It might be a good idea for the baby-sitter to have control of the reward and give it to Billy once the temper tantrum has been ignored and he has been quiet. This reinforcement might be more TV time, special treats such as ice cream and cake, etc. The parents could also make a large chart and Billy could get a star for behaving himself when they have gone. The star could be traded the next day for some special type of reward given by the parents.

Answer 7: Again, the parent should make some estimate how long the temper tantrums last or have been lasting in the past. They should then ask the baby-sitter how long he continues yelling after they have left, to determine whether this is decreasing each Saturday night. The parents could also speed up the process by soliciting the baby-sitter's help in coming over more often for practice sessions, rather than waiting until Saturday.

CASE NUMBER 3

Jimmy, age eight, is really a pretty good boy. He is happy, loving, respectful, etc. His only real problem behavior seems to be a complete failure to hang up his clothes. They are found constantly littered around the floor of his bedroom. In the usual situation, Jimmy rushes home from school, heads quickly towards his bedroom, changes his clothes while tossing his school clothes on the floor. He then grabs his football, heads for the door and is seen again about dinnertime. Usually while this is going on, mother is saying, "Hang up your clothes, please, Jimmy." Jimmy replies, "OK," but rarely, if ever, does what is requested of him. Again, the problem is not meanness or orneriness; it is really just a little bit of forgetfulness. Often mother comes into the room and cleans them up herself, or perhaps yells at Jimmy a little when he returns.

Case Number 3—Questions

Question 1: What is the behavior that you wish to eliminate, and what is the behavior you wish to develop?
Question 2: What do you think the reinforcement is for this behavior?
Question 3: Describe the program you might use to handle this problem and how you would evaluate it.

Case Number 3—Answers

Answer 1: Throwing clothes on the floor should be eliminated and hanging them in the closet should be reinforced.

Answer 2: This is a somewhat tricky situation, since there really may not be any direct and positive reinforcement for this behavior. The reinforcements are really an avoidance of the "work" of hanging up the clothes and of losing the time it would take when Jimmy wants to go outside and play. Mother also may pick them up herself.

Answer 3: The main criteria for any program should be that it attaches some direct positive reinforcement for the acceptable behavior of hanging up the clothes. For example, if Jimmy earns an allowance, a portion of this can be used to pay him every day for hanging up his clothing, or he can earn extra "staying up" time. If possible, playing football could only be done *if* the clothes are hung up.

There should be a definite "check-up" time in which mother (with Jimmy there) evaluates the job and awards reinforcement. Evaluations can be done by beginning a check-up time in which the number of items of clothing lying on the floor are recorded. This could be begun a few days before the treatment program and then continued throughout.

Chapter 6

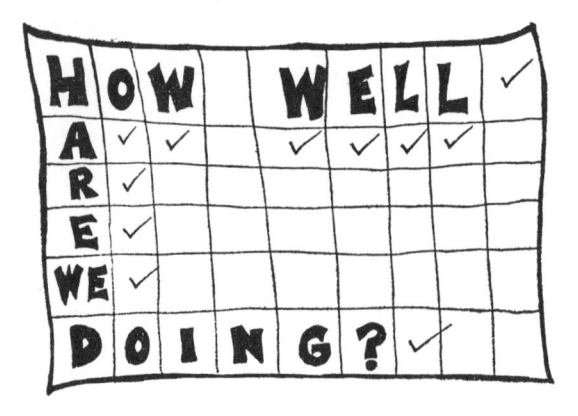

HOW ARE WE DOING?

WE HAVE ALL HEARD the expression, "You cannot see the forest for the trees." The thought behind this age-old expression applies equally well to a learning situation as it does to many other situations in our life. Too often, because we are so close to the child whom we are trying to teach, we are unable to discern that learning is occurring. Consequently then, we need to measure periodically the effect of our teaching.

Teachers in school rooms do this all the time. Each of us can recall those terrible things known as exams. What were the purposes of these exams? These were designed to tell the teacher (and also to tell our parents via a report card) how well we were progressing in our school learning. The exam was a sampling of what the teacher had taught and what we were supposed to have learned. How well we performed on exams indicated to the teacher how much we had learned. More important, to the good teacher an exam indicated what parts of the curriculum he had failed to teach well.

And so it is with you and your child in the home. You need to assess periodically whether or not the child is learning what you want him to learn. The examinations we recommend to parents, however, are not the type that you took in school. In fact, they are really not examinations at all, but a daily *record* of how well the child is performing. A good example of why it might be well to keep daily records, why a parent sometimes is unable to "see the forest for the trees," occurs when the parent begins the process of toilet training the child. This often times is a very difficult and trying period, probably more so in the case of a handicapped child than with a normal child. We find two things happening during this toilet training period— first, parents tend to become overly optimistic about the first few isolated successes of bowel movements or urinations which occur on the toilet as opposed to in the diaper. Second, we find other parents who become discouraged, oftentimes unduly, at the number of times the child wets his diapers instead of urinating in the toilet. Because this is a behavior which the parent deals with many times during the day, it is oftentimes difficult for her to assess properly whether any improvement is occurring. (Thus, a record should probably be maintained.)

A toilet training record might take the form of the chart shown. This chart is shown for a 15-day period. Each day is broken down into half-hour periods. The parent records using the two symbols of circles and triangles. A triangle indicates a bowel movement; a circle indicates a urination. If the bowel movement occurs in the toilet as opposed to in the diaper, the triangle is placed on the chart with no other marking. If the bowel movement, however, occurs in the diaper, a triangle is placed on the chart with an "X" within it. The same system is used for urination. A circle on the chart without the "X" indicates that the urination occurred on the potty. But a circle with an "X" indicates that urination occurred in the diaper. An X on the chart without any other mark indicates that the child was placed on the potty but without result. A count each day of the number of bowel movements and the number of urinations which occurred in the toilet as opposed to in the diaper will give a daily record of how well the child is performing. A detailed examination of the chart would show some success beginning to occur. Also, a pattern is emerging, which

70   *Isn't It Time He Outgrew This?*

TOILET TRAINING CHART

△ = Bowel Movement in Toilet ○ = Urination in Toilet
▲ = Bowel Movement   ⊗ = Urination
                              X = Child on Potty; No Results

	1	2	3	4	5	6	7	8	9	10	11	12	13	14	15
7:00 – 7:30	⊗	⊗	⊗	⊗	⊗	⊗	⊗	⊗	△⊗	⊗	⊗	⊗	△⊗	⊗	⊗
7:31 – 8:00				▲	X	△	X	△		△	X	X		△	X
8:01 – 8:30	⊗	△	△			△		⊗		△	△	⊗	X		
8:31 – 9:00	▲				X	⊗				⊗			X	⊗	
9:01 – 9:30					▲			⊗	▲			⊗	⊗	⊗	
9:31 – 10:00		⊗		○	⊗										
10:01 – 10:30	⊗							⊗	⊗	○		▲		⊗	X
10:31 – 11:00				▲⊗	⊗										
11:01 – 11:30									▲						
11:31 – 12:00					⊗			⊗			⊗	○	△	X	X
12:01 – 12:30		▲	⊗		▲	▲⊗	○	X	X	△○	X	X		△	△
12:31 – 1:00			○					△	X		▲		⊗		⊗
1:01 – 1:30	▲⊗								⊗			⊗		⊗	
1:31 – 2:00					⊗			⊗		⊗	⊗				
2:01 – 2:30					⊗		⊗					⊗			⊗
2:31 – 3:00		⊗	⊗	▲						⊗	⊗		⊗		
3:01 – 3:30					⊗			⊗	△	△	X	△	X	X	△
3:31 – 4:00	▲⊗	▲	△		△	○	X	X	⊗		△		△	△	⊗
4:01 – 4:30		⊗		⊗				⊗	△		⊗		⊗	X	
4:31 – 5:00					⊗	⊗	▲		⊗		⊗		X	⊗	
5:01 – 5:30	⊗		⊗					⊗				⊗			
5:31 – 6:00					⊗		⊗			⊗					
6:01 – 6:30		⊗	▲	△	X				△	X	X	△	X	○	X
6:31 – 7:00					△		⊗	⊗	⊗		△	⊗	⊗		
7:01 – 7:30	▲⊗			⊗	⊗	○		▲		⊗					⊗
7:31 – 8:00															

How Well Are We Doing?

tells the mother when to put the child on the potty.

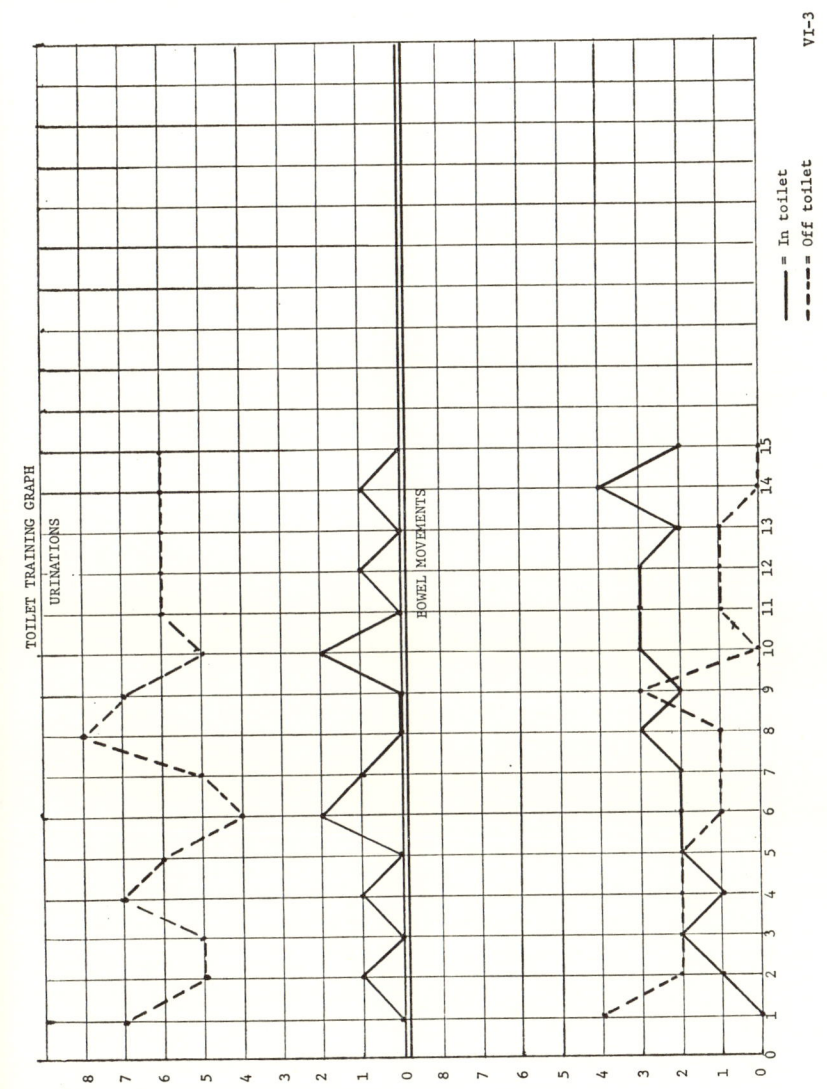

This record would be even more graphic if we transferred this information to a simple graph. The graph shows the child's performance during the first month of toilet training. As you look at the graph you see that there is very little improvement in the number of urinations occurring on the toilet as opposed to in the diaper. On the other hand, the child has reduced the average number of bowel movements from the beginning of the month from about two to four daily in the diaper to almost none in the diaper and has increased those in the toilet from none to around approximately two to four. Thus we might say, by looking at this graph, that the child is definitely showing improvement in his bowel movement training, but still has not yet shown progress in his urination training. *The parent who is faced with this situation daily could well have become discouraged because of the constant wet diapers and have failed to overlook the improvement which was occurring in the bowel movement training.* Relying entirely on your memory can cause problems!

Now let us turn our attention to Billy and his temper tantrums. Temper tantrums, as we have shown, are traumatic experiences for both parents and children. Parents tend to become extremely upset with the child who has repeated temper tantrums.

These oftentimes, even though they may occur only once or twice a day, are magnified out of proportion and become obstacles to any further learning. It becomes rather important to the parent to know whether or not they are succeeding in reducing the number of temper tantrums. Therefore, a record is needed.

A number of techniques for keeping this record might be suggested. For instance, the mother might keep a chart posted on her refrigerator door in which she has nothing more than the days of the month labeled down the left-hand column. A pencil is kept near at hand; everytime the child has a temper tantrum, a mark is placed next to the day of the month. Such a record for thirty-one days is illustrated. At the end of the day, the parent can count the number of marks she has made next to that date and record that number in the right-hand column and thus she will have a daily record of the number of temper tantrums. As with the toilet training, an examination of this record, or a charting of it, would illustrate quite well to the parent whether or not these temper tantrums are

How Well Are We Doing?

Number of Temper Tantrums

1. ✓✓✓✓
2. ✓✓✓✓✓✓
3. ✓✓✓✓
4. ✓✓✓✓✓
5. ✓✓✓✓✓
6. ✓✓✓✓
7. ✓✓✓✓
8. ✓✓✓✓✓
9. ✓✓✓✓
10. ✓✓✓
11. ✓✓✓✓✓
12. ✓✓✓✓
13. ✓✓✓✓
14. ✓✓✓✓
15. ✓✓✓✓
16. ✓✓✓
17. ✓✓✓
18. ✓✓✓✓
19. ✓✓✓
20. ✓✓✓✓✓
21. ✓✓✓✓
22. ✓✓✓
23. ✓✓
24. ✓✓✓
25. ✓✓✓✓
26. ✓✓✓
27. ✓✓
28. ✓✓
29. ✓✓
30. ✓✓
31. ✓✓

✓ = Temper Tantrum

being reduced as the days and weeks pass by. In the illustration the parent can see some improvement in that the number of tantrums per day has been reduced to two in the last five days of the period. The parent, however, might well have reached a conclusion that no improvement was being shown because tantrums were still occurring.

The types of records we have talked about up to this point are those which indicate the number of times a certain event occurs namely, bowel movements, urinations or temper tantrums. There are other types of records. If we are trying, for instance, to teach a child the differences between the color red and the color yellow, we might record the number of times he was able to identify correctly those colors and we might also record the number of times that he was unable to identify the colors. This relationship between right and wrong would show whether or not his ability to recognize the colors was improving. This relationship between right and wrong is very similar to the relationship of right and wrong answers that we made on examinations which our teachers gave us. We knew that if we had 90 percent right answers, this was a rather good performance. So it would be with the child who was trying to distinguish between red and yellow. If he were correct 50 percent of the time, this would be quite poor performance. In fact, he could achieve this performance merely by guessing. If, on the other hand, he were able to achieve 90 percent correct, we would probably say this was quite good. However, in this particular task, we might designate 100 percent as our criterion for success.

There is still another type of record. Many of the things that we do in our society we must perform at a fairly rapid rate. Therefore, how many times we are able to do a thing in a set period of time may become quite important.

Imagine if you will the case of the stenographer who has recently been employed in the Ring-a-Ding Marble and Agate Company. It soon becomes obvious that her rate of typing is 20 words per minute. Unfortunately for our heroine, her time on the job will be short-lived for the Ring-a-Ding Marble and Agate Company needs a girl who can type at least 60 words a minute to keep up with the volume of letters which the busy producers of marbles and agates dictate each day. They could have saved themselves and the young lady much grief if they had taken some samples of her speed in typing before they hired her. Such samples or records of how many times a person can do something per minute is called "rate data."

An example of a learning task of this type might be counting how fast a child can put the pieces of a puzzle together. For instance, if it takes the child 10 minutes to put together 10 pieces in a puzzle, we can say that he is putting in the pieces of the puzzle at the rate of one per minute. If, on the other hand, it takes him but five minutes to put in the 10 pieces of the puzzle, we are able to say that he is putting in the pieces of the puzzle at the rate of two per minute. Thus we find that rate data is found by dividing the number of times the thing is done by the number of minutes which it took to do it. In the two examples listed above, the child who did 10 pieces in 10 minutes, the 10 was divided by 10 which gave us a rate of one per minute. In the case of the child who did 10 pieces in five minutes, the 10 pieces were divided by the five minutes which gave us a rate of two pieces per minute. Many manipulative tasks are suitable for these types of records.

Parents and teachers, therefore, should be capable of not only keeping straight counts as in the case of urinations, bowel movements or temper tantrums, and the number of right as opposed to the number of wrong, as in the case of color discrimination, but also they should know how to record the number of times that a child can do something in a set period of time and then be able to reduce these figures to rate per minute. All of these are forms of records which will tell how well the child is doing.

Let us hasten to say, however, that we do not keep the records just for the sake of record keeping. The records let us know how well the child is learning or better still, how we are teaching. Remember—we do know that handicapped children can learn. If they are not learning, it is not the child's fault. We maintain that the teacher has not yet found the proper combinations of cues and reinforcements or perhaps has not broken the behavior down into small enough parts.

Therefore, the record tells us how well we are teaching, and tells us whether or not the combination of cue, behavior and reinforcement is succeeding. If the record tells us that the child is not learning, it is time then to change our approach. We do this by changing one element at a time. Perhaps we might break the behavior down to smaller steps and then provide the cue and the reinforcement to accomplish that smaller step. On the other hand, perhaps the behavior is refined to a very small step and cannot really be broken down much further. It is then time to change either the cue or the reinforcement, keep further records for a period of three to seven trials or days and determine whether or not improvement is occurring. If not, it is time to change again.

The purpose of the record, therefore, is to give us reinforcement or feedback that tells us how well we are doing as teachers. If the record says that learning is not occurring, we must then say we are not doing well as teachers and we must change what we are doing. We should make a notation on our record and indicate the type of change that we are making. For instance, in the case of the child learning to discriminate between red and yellow, we might change the reinforcement from social reinforcement to primary reinforcement for each correct answer. The type of changes we make will be dependent upon what we know about the child.

There is another advantage to the record. It tells us what types of things have succeeded in the past. When we accumulate this type of record we are then able to teach more efficiently, in that we will know the types of cues or materials that most appeal to the child and what type of reinforcements are most pleasing to him.

Thus we see that record keeping is quite different than the old report card and examination period which we remember as children. The record is not so much to tell the child how well he is doing; he will be told that through the reinforcement that he is receiving in the daily learning task. The record and the examination, however, is to tell us how well we are teaching and what changes we should make so that the child can learn. The record is our report card.

It is time now for a little practice session. Choose your favorite comedians on television. Arrange your schedule so that you can watch three different comedians in one week. As you watch each of them, count the number of times the audience bursts into laughter after the comedian utters a punch line. Also, record the number of minutes during which you observe the comedian. At the conclusion of the observation, divide the number of minutes into the number of times you recorded the laughter. This will give you a laugh rate for each comedian. A comparison of this laugh rate will then allow you to make such profound observations as to which comedian was the funniest that week because he produced more spontaneous laughter among his audience.

Chapter 7

SELF-HELP SKILLS

This chapter is to serve as an introduction to all the following chapters that deal with the various self-help skills. All the chapters will be arranged in the same manner as this one. What we hope to do here is to give you some general directions and guidelines to keep in mind when teaching your child these skills. After you have read this chapter, you can turn to the chapter that deals with the self-help skill that you want to teach first.

PINPOINTING THE BEHAVIOR

ONE OF THE MOST frequent mistakes that we find parents making is that they often begin trying to teach a large chunk of BEHAVIOR instead of a small piece of behavior. Even before you begin the first teaching lesson with your child, you should have decided exactly what step in the skill you are going to teach first. Each skill presented in the chapter has been broken down by us into steps in the order of their occurrence. You should test your child by having him do each step in order until you reach the point where he begins having trouble. Then you begin the actual teaching by starting at the beginning and proceed with the steps he already knows—reinforcing him as you go along. You should be prepared to utilize exaggerated cues, reinforcement and all the special techniques we shall show you at the point where he begins learning the *new* step.

If your testing shows that he cannot do the first step in the series then you may want to consider using the reverse chaining procedures we have discussed previously.

CUES

Begin by selecting a quiet part of the house where you are not likely to be disturbed. If possible, arrange for someone else

Self-Help Skills

to answer the phone and door and to handle anything that might disturb your sessions.

VERBAL CUES

In the chapter on "Cues," we presented the verbal cues that accompany each of the steps in shoe-tying. These are usually one or two word directions which describe the action required of your child—"Pull," "Push," etc. In the following chapters, we shall present the verbal cues we have found successful along with their matching behaviors. You may wish to adapt these, however, to fit the names that your child may use for these concepts. Always be sure to give the simplest cue that adequately describes the behavior you want. Also, try to limit other conversation and concentrate upon the spoken cues and reinforcements.

EXAGGERATED CUES

Also, in the following chapters we shall present what we have been calling "exaggerated cues" or child cues. If you find that the part of dressing that your child finds difficult is buttoning, then you may want to have him learn buttoning with very large buttons. If his clothing does not have large buttons, your winter coats usually do. Large zippers are also good. Your child might have more success by beginning to tie his father's shoes and then his older brother's, and finally his. This is the same principle your first grade teacher probably used to teach you how to write. At that age you were using pencils the size of small baseball bats and writing on paper with lines six inches apart. As you progressed, the pencils and the space between the lines got smaller and writing became more natural. We think that teachers have had a good idea all along and we want to follow through on it.

REINFORCEMENT

Eventually children learn to dress themselves, by themselves, without needing adult encouragement. They learn what clothing they like, how it looks, what goes together, etc. These

ADULT REINFORCEMENTS will be strong enough eventually to maintain that behavior. The same is true for all the other skills. Eventually the child will perform them by himself.

These REINFORCEMENTS are not strong enough right now to use at the beginning of training. So you should decide what child reinforcements or what combination of reinforcements are strong enough now to get the job done. You may want to use candy or fruit cereal bits as added reinforcement. Whatever you decide to use, *always* pair that reinforcement with a spoken and a social reinforcement—a smile, a "good boy," a hug, a pat on the back. These are the most powerful reinforcements we have to offer. The trick is to use these as efficiently and as effectively as we can. That means giving them immediately after the desired behavior and only then.

We have found that using candy or a cereal bit not only helps the child, but it also helps the parent. An M&M® is small; it is easy to give quickly after a behavior. You are also less likely to give candy to a child who has just made a mistake. If you can give your social reinforcements as effectively and at the same time you give the cereal bit, you will find the cereal bit helps to guide *your* behavior, too. When both you and the child can get along without the cereal bits, then it is time to begin fading them out gradually over a period of time.

We also believe that spoken reinforcement and cues serve another purpose. A child will eventually learn to perform on his own the self-help skill you have been teaching. As he begins to perform the skill independently, you will hear him repeating to himself what you have said to cue and reinforce his behavior. You may notice that when your child begins working by himself he will say "Good boy!" to himself, or he may repeat the verbal cues that you used. We feel that this is an essential step in the maturation of your child and another good reason for the use of social and verbal reinforcements.

SPECIAL TECHNIQUES

Behavior problems often occur in the course of teaching these skills to your child. As you begin to demand performance from him, you may find some initial refusals. Each chapter tells how to adapt behavioral techniques to the given teaching situation. But whether you are teaching eating, dressing or washing of hands, the underlying principles are the same. Refusals are best met by removing the teaching materials and turning your back for a short time. This simply removes any possible reinforcement from the child and indicates that you are not going to bargain with him or attempt to persuade him to work. After fifteen or thirty seconds, return the materials and repeat the request that first led to the refusal. If he again refuses, repeat the procedure. If you are consistent, and you have chosen strong reinforcements, he will eventually comply with your request and this compliance should be strongly reinforced.

It is also a good idea to have some special event follow the completion of each day's training session. A special event does not have to be anything more than an opportunity for your child to have the undivided attention of both parents. If you make the event seem important, he will believe it is important, too. The event happens *only* after the completion of a training session.

It may happen that you and your child reach a stand-off and he refuses to perform anymore. In that case it is best to end the session *and* withhold the special event. You might review your training session and ask yourself if you were requiring too complex a task from your child or if you were fading out the candy or cereal bits too soon. If so you may want to modify your approach. If the problem is "just plain stubbornness," resume the training the next day as scheduled. Sometimes it may be obvious that missing the special event has caused your child to see immediately the error of his ways. In that case you may wish to resume the training that same day and give your child the chance to redeem himself.

KEEPING TRACK

In each chapter, we shall show simple and direct ways to keep track of what is happening and how well your child is doing. We believe these charts and graphs are important, because they tell you how well you are doing and how well your child is doing. They tell you when it is time to move onto the next step in the skill or when you may have moved too fast and need to back up a step. We are sure that you will find they are not such a bother after all and are worth the small amount of time they require.

Now decide what skill you want to teach first and turn to that chapter.

Chapter 8

"USE YOUR SPOON, HARRY!"
or
How to Teach Your Child to Feed Himself

IN OUR EXPERIENCE of working with parents of handicapped children, we find that the area in which most parents achieve a great deal of success in utilizing behavior modification procedures is when they teach their child to eat. Most parents specify this, along with toilet training, as one of the two most basic skills which they wish their child to learn first. Toilet training sometimes can be a discouraging task but teaching a child to eat can be accomplished rapidly and with a great deal of success. And so, we recommend to you parents that if you are just starting out with your handicapped child and are prepared to utilize the procedures we recommend in this book and your child has not yet learned to feed himself that you start by teaching him to feed himself.

The procedures which follow are certainly not meant to be all-inclusive. Yet we believe that they include examples of types of situations in which you may find yourself when teaching your handicapped child. We hope that the information presented will give you a guide as to how to proceed.

PINPOINTING AND ANALYZING THE BEHAVIOR

The ultimate objective, of course, is to have the child feed himself using a knife, a fork, a spoon and to be able to handle these as an adult or a "normal" child. Being able to use all three of these utensils in eating an entire meal constitutes a complex BEHAVIOR. As we shall see, using any one of these also is a complex BEHAVIOR, and so we shall begin by narrowing our choice of these complex BEHAVIORS to the child being able to use a spoon to feed himself.

However, even before he is able to reach this stage, a child will usually pick up food and eat with his fingers. Finger feeding should be encouraged to teach the child the amount of food he should put in his mouth at one time and to help him develop proper chewing habits. The child should be required to pick up one item of food at a time. He should be taught not to pick up another piece until he has eaten the first one. This can be accomplished by placing the food on the child's tray only one piece at a time initially and then gradually expanding the number of pieces placed on the child's tray. Only food that is appropriate finger food should be used. Baby Vienna sausage, cereal bits and cookies are very suitable.

CUES

When teaching a retarded child how to feed himself, we strongly recommend that this not be done with the remainder of the family present. In fact, there should be as few distractions as possible. Learning to feed himself is similar to any other learning activity and should be done where there is a minimum of distraction.

A mother must accept the fact that when her retarded child, or any child for that matter, is learning to eat food will be spilled. This tends to upset some mothers. If such is the case, it is recommended that the child be covered with a plastic bib and that the floor also be covered with newspapers which can be easily picked up.

The feeding area is prepared the same way for each feeding learning session. The child will use his spoon, his dish, his cup. He will sit in his chair with his bib on. These, in effect, become the cues which ready him to eat. As we shall see in the section entitled "chaining," other cues will be presented, depending on how well the child can manipulate the spoon.

REINFORCEMENT

It should be obvious to the parent that when teaching the child to eat, the food itself is serving as a primary reinforcement; therefore, it is important when teaching a child how to feed himself that you use foods that he likes. In fact, using such foods as applesauce, ice cream, fruit cocktail—depending on the individual child—would probably be quite effective.

When teaching a child to feed himself, the primary reinforcement (food) can never be faded out although less desirable foods will gradually have to be substituted for the more palatable goodies. In fact, this is an excellent way to teach a child to accept new and more adult foods. Intersperse a new food with a more desirable child-food. For instance, mix peas (definitely an adult food) with applesauce. Initially the bulk of the mixture will be applesauce but gradually the amount of peas will be increased until over a period of time the entire mixture is peas.

As you recall from the chapter on reinforcement, primary reinforcement must be accompanied by social reinforcement. The social reinforcement can be gradually faded out as the child becomes more proficient with the use of the spoon. In the initial learning stages it is important to reinforce him socially with every mouthful. In the later stages social reinforcement may occur every second, third or fourth mouthful. Gradually by the time the child is able to scoop the food himself and deliver it to his mouth the social reinforcement may be omitted almost entirely during meal times but should be delivered at the conclusion of the meal.

CHAINING

Once a child is feeding himself adequately using his fingers, he is ready to learn how to feed himself using a spoon. We teach him to use a spoon by reverse chaining, a technique you have met before. Reverse chaining is starting at the end and working towards the beginning. In feeding, the end goal is putting the food in the mouth.

One starts to teach a child to feed himself with a spoon utilizing the reverse chain method by placing your hand over the child's hand as he grasps the spoon. Scoop the food and take the food to his mouth. Initially with each mouthful of food the parent is telling the child "Good," "Very Good," or any other approving, reinforcing words. Pats on the shoulder or gentle pats on the head are appropriate as other signs of social reinforcement as he eats the food. After you have practiced guiding the child's hand all the way to his mouth and back to the bowl a number of times, you are ready to scoop the food with the child and guide the spoon almost to his mouth. Release the child's hand and let him take the food the rest of the way into his mouth. Try this a number of times. If the child is unable to put the food in his mouth, you must examine how far from the mouth you are releasing the child's hand; perhaps you must guide the hand closer to the mouth before you release it. Perhaps he may even need more practice and more guidance with just the motion from bowl to mouth. The important thing is to allow the child to have success when you

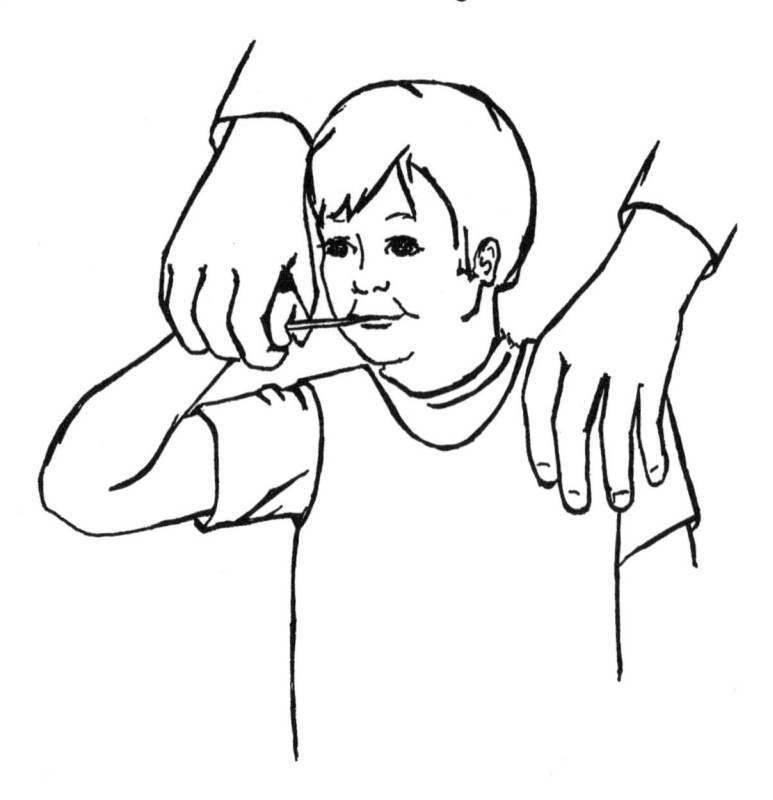

"Use Your Spoon, Harry!"

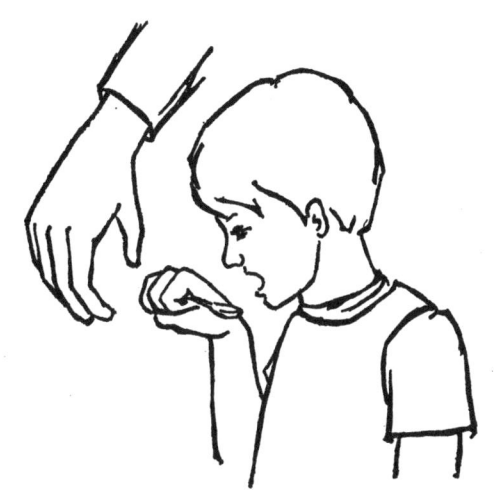

release his hand and the hand moves the food independently to the mouth.

The parent gradually releases the child's hand further and further from the mouth. Notice the illustrations which illustrate possible distances from the child's mouth that the parent might release the child's hand as he progresses through the reverse chain learning procedure.

The last thing the child learns to do is to scoop the food by himself.

EXTINCTION

Inappropriate behavior while feeding can take many forms. The technique to eliminate this behavior as you have learned before is known as extinction. On a day to day basis, inappropriate behavior such as playing with food, spitting food or crying is stopped by removing the food from the child when he starts exhibiting this behavior. This is known as "TIME OUT"—you take the food from him (you are removing the opportunity for him to get a primary reinforcer) and then you ignore him (and thus remove from him the opportunity to get socially reinforced). "TIME OUT" therefore is removing the opportunity for reinforcement.

You should *not* spend any time nagging the child. After a period of time, return the food. If the child is fussing or crying, do not return the food to him until he stops. You may have to remove the food a number of times before you extinguish inappropriate behavior.

Oftentimes you will be faced with a child who refuses to eat although his behavior in refusing to eat is really not bad in that he does not play with the food, he does not spit it, nor does he cry. In these cases, the technique is to leave the food

with the child as long as he does not play with it. Ignore him when he is not eating. To keep this from being an endless stand-off, establish a precise time limit. A kitchen timer is very useful for this. If the child still continues not to eat, remove the food from the child permanently for this meal; take the child down from his chair and let him resume other activities. In order to teach the child proper eating behavior, it is sometimes better to let the child miss a meal or a part of a meal. This will not cause him to suffer from malnutrition. It will in the long run save the mother and the child much difficulty at the table. The mother will find that the child will accept new food and conduct himself properly at the table so that he can eat with the family, with company, or go with the family to a restaurant.

SPECIAL TECHNIQUES

When teaching a child to feed himself, one must be very careful of some of the cues chosen—in this case, eating utensils, bibs and cups.

Regarding bibs, the bib shown below is strongly recommended. The plastic catch-all which is part of the bib is *nonflexible* and is very effective in catching food that the child loses from his spoon and from his mouth.

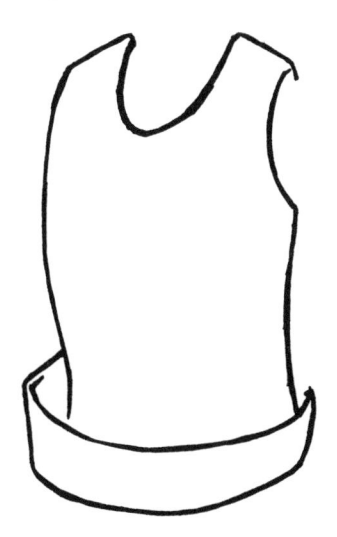

The choice of eating utensils for the handicapped child should be no different than for a "normal" child. Child sized utensils are especially recommended. However, if your child has physical disabilities, it may be necessary to have specially constructed eating utensils when teaching the child to feed himself.

Pictured is one of a number of types of utensils which can be used by physically handicapped children. The parent must first determine what the range of motion of the child's limbs is. Once having made that determination, the parent must choose the modified utensil which will most compensate for the limited limb motion.

Even if special utensils are not required, it is often necessary to enlarge the handle of a utensil to allow the child to hold it more easily. Any artificial enlargement should be considered a temporary measure. As soon as possible the child should be encouraged to use the utensil without this additional aid.

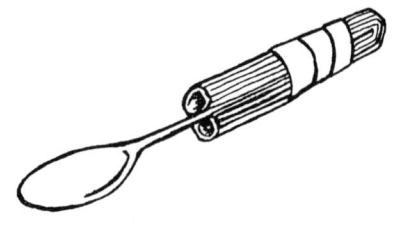

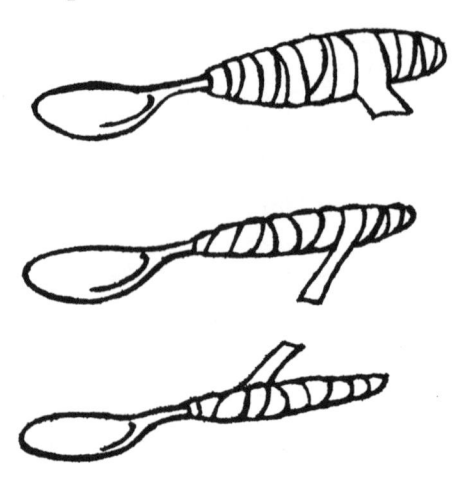

Enlarging the handle can be done in a variety of ways. One simple technique is to cut the handle from a bleach bottle and insert the spoon in the handle. Another way to enlarge the handle is to tape rubber tubing to the spoon which can be removed after the child develops sufficient grasp to hold the spoon. Taping the handle of the spoon allows an artificial enlargement of the spoon and also an easy way to gradually reduce the size of the handle. The tape can be removed in stages until the spoon is back to its normal size.

SPECIAL TECHNIQUES

The choice of a cup from which the child is to learn how to drink is quite important. It might be helpful if the cup contained a plastic cover. The one pictured here has a nozzle

similar to a nipple which might be ideal for the child still drinking from a bottle. The child should be weaned from this nipple-type cap as soon as possible and given another type of plastic cap over the glass to be used. This cap has a small hole. Gradually this hole can be widened by cutting out the top of it and allowing more fluid to pour through it. As soon as the child has practiced with this so that he does not spill, the hole can be made wider until eventually the cap can be removed from the cup altogether.

CASE EXAMPLE

Case 1

Jimmy is one and a half years old and is beginning to learn how to eat. His mother desires him to eat finger food at first and has chosen an appropriate cereal which she knows that Jimmy likes. She wishes him to be able to eat the food with his fingers. However, when she puts the chunks of cereal on his tray he grabs them in his fists and stuffs three to five at a time in his mouth.

Please describe the behavior you would like to change.

What is the cue or situation that seems to set off the behavior?

What do you think is reinforcing this behavior?

What incompatible behavior would you develop?

What cues would you provide to assist in developing this incompatible behavior?

How could you measure whether you were having any success?

POSSIBLE SOLUTIONS TO CASE EXAMPLES

Case I

Please describe the behavior you would like to change. The behavior which we would like to change in the case of Jimmy is to have him stop picking up three to five chunks of cereal at a time and stuffing them all in his mouth. We desire him to pick up one piece of cereal at a time and place it in his mouth.

What is the cue or situation that seems to set off the behavior? The cue or situation that seems to set off the behavior is the placing on the tray a number of chunks of cereal.

What do you think is reinforcing this behavior? You will notice that the mother has chosen a cereal which she knows that Jimmy likes. Therefore, we must assume that the taste of the cereal becomes a primary reinforcement for the child and he desires to stuff as much of it as he can into his mouth at one time.

What incompatible behavior would you develop? The behavior which is incompatible to stuffing three to five at a time in his mouth is placing only one cereal chunk in his mouth at a time.

What cues would you provide to assist in developing this

incompatible behavior? We indicated that the cues which were causing the child to stuff three to five chunks of cereal in his mouth at a time was the placing of a number of chunks of cereal on the tray at one time. Therefore to assist in developing the behavior of placing only one chunk in his mouth at a time, initially only place one chunk of cereal on the tray at one time. When the child is used to placing this piece of cereal in his mouth, then place two pieces and keep his hands from picking up both pieces at one time. Then gradually extend the number of pieces of cereal that you are placing on the tray.

How could you measure whether you were having any success? The measurement of whether or not success is being achieved in this case is whether or not the child is picking up one piece of cereal at a time. A situation which will be initially presented to him, that is, presenting him only one piece of cereal at a time will allow him to achieve the success. When we move to the stage of two pieces of cereal at a time we should observe whether or not the child will just pick up one piece and eat it and then the second piece and eat it or whether he will try to grab both pieces at the same time. If he tries to grab both pieces at the same time, prevent his hand from taking the second piece, but allow his hand to take the first piece. Do this a number of times and then once again expose the two pieces to him to see if he has learned to take one piece at a time. When you are confident that he takes only one piece at a time with two pieces exposed, place three pieces on the tray and so on until you can place a number of pieces on the tray and he chooses only one at a time.

Case II

Susan is three years old and has learned to feed herself. However, when her mother now presents to her food which is not her favorite, she takes her spoon and bangs at the food squirting it all over the table and all over her mother and her brother who sits on the other side of her. Everytime it happens, the brother yells at her and tells her to stop doing that, and the father immediately also yells at Susan and tells her to stop it. Mother tries to hold Susan's hand and quietly tells Susan to stop banging and start eating. Sometimes Susan does but most often she continues to bang away at the food until the mother is forced to feed her.

>Please describe the behavior you would like to change.
>What is the cue or situation that seems to set off the behavior?
>What do you think is reinforcing this behavior?
>Do you think the parent is being reinforced as well? How?
>How would you remove, cut off or eliminate the reinforcement that you think is maintaining the behavior?
>What incompatible behavior would you develop?
>What techniques would you use to develop this incompatible behavior?
>How could you measure whether you are having any success?

Case II

Please describe the behavior you would like to change. The behavior that we would like to change in this case is Susan banging at her food and squirting it all over the table and all over her mother and brother who sit on either side of her.

What is the cue or situation that seems to set off the behavior? Behavior occurs when Susan is presented food which she does not like.

What do you think is reinforcing this behavior? When Susan bangs at the food and squirts it all over the table a number of things occur: her brother yells at her, her father yells at her and her mother quietly tells Susan to stop banging. It is difficult to imagine that the yelling by both the brother and the father are reinforcing, although they may well be, for they are providing Susan much attention. We can safely assume however, that mother holding Susan's hand and quietly talking to her and then feeding her might be very reinforcing behavior for a child.

Do you think the parent is being reinforced as well? How? Susan's mother is probably being reinforced when she stops Susan from banging in that she is ceasing a disturbance at the table which is obviously upsetting the whole family. Moreover, being a mother, she is concerned with the child eating properly and so consequently she will feed the child and then be pleased that the child has taken the food from her.

How would you remove, cut off or eliminate the reinforcement that you think is maintaining the behavior? As with any child there should be only one teacher. So the first thing that this family must determine is who is going to correct Susan at the table. Since mother sits next to her, it probably should be her task to conduct the correction and the teaching of Susan. As soon as Susan starts to bang her food the food should be removed from her and she should be ignored or placed in a "time out" situation. Thus, any reinforcement for her banging would be stopped.

What incompatible behavior would you develop? The incompatible behavior which we wish to develop in this case is Susan taking her spoon and eating properly. If she is doing that she cannot bang at the food.

What techniques would you use to develop this incompatible behavior? You will notice that one of the cues which seems to be causing this behavior to occur is the presentation of food which is not liked by Susan. Therefore, we must slowly help Susan develop a taste for that food. We do this by presenting food which she does like and, when she eats that properly, mixing that food that is liked with a small amount of food that is not liked. You will recall in the chapter you have just read that we use the example of mixing applesauce and peas. We assumed that applesauce was liked by the child. We knew that peas were not. Therefore, in trying to get the child to eat peas we initially introduced only a small amount of peas mixed with the applesauce. With each new serving of applesauce we increased the amount of peas until gradually over a period of time the amount of peas exceeded that of applesauce. Gradually the applesauce could be eliminated entirely.

In addition, the mother must remember that if Susan begins to bang at the table with her eating utensils or causes other such disturbances the eating utensils and the food must be removed from Susan. When Susan finally quiets, then the eating utensils and the food may be returned to Susan. Should she then reinaugurate her disturbance, the food once again is removed. Susan is allowed to have her food in front of her only when her behavior is appropriate.

How could you measure whether you are having any success? There are two measurements involved here. One is the gradual introduction of the peas into the applesauce, or the unlike food into that which is liked. The parent should keep careful track of the mixture that she is providing the child. Initially the child will eat predominately food that she likes. Gradually a little more of the disliked food will be added, perhaps a spoon or two, and the parent will note whether the child eats that properly. If the child does, the parent then should perhaps add another half a spoon or another spoonful to the mixture at the next feeding.

The other measurement that must be taken in this case is a count of Susan's food banging behavior. We already know that she bangs her food that she does not like. We should count the number of times she does this and how many times we must remove the food from her during the meal. We should chart this and retain this count so that we can compare it with counts that we shall take at future meals. If the number of times that we are removing the food from Susan because of her inappropriate behavior is decreasing, we obviously are having success.

Case III

Jimmy is learning how to feed himself. His mother is teaching him to feed himself by using a reverse chain procedure. However, she seems to have run into difficulty. She has been succeeding quite well when she helped Jimmy scoop the food with his spoon and took his hand about three-quarters of the way to his mouth. He was able to move the hand quite well into his mouth and seemed to enjoy the process. Now his mother is releasing his hand about half way to his mouth and he is able to get the spoon to his mouth only about one half of the time. The mother feels that she is unable to get him past this stage.

>Please describe the behavior you would like to change.
>What is the cue or situation that seems to set off the behavior?
>What would you do now to help this mother achieve success?
>How could you measure whether you are having any success?

Case III

Please describe the behavior you would like to change. We should like to have Jimmy have success in getting the spoon to his mouth when his mother releases his hand about halfway to his mouth.

What is the cue or situation that seems to set off the behavior? The cue or situation that sets off the behavior in this case is the releasing of Jimmy's hand when it is halfway to his mouth.

What would you do now to help this mother achieve success? This mother had achieved success when she was releasing Jimmy's hand when it was about three-quarters of the way to his mouth. When she moved to the next stage, which was releasing his hand when it was about halfway to his mouth, Jimmy is only enjoying success about one-half of the time. We might, therefore, assume that the jump between three-quarters of the way to his mouth and one-half of the way to his mouth is too big a step for Jimmy to take. We should begin by going back to three-quarters of the way from Jimmy's mouth and releasing the spoon at that level to allow Jimmy success in feeding himself once again. We should then take his hand and release it about an inch or two below that point and allow Jimmy to have success at that level. Then gradually release it an inch at a time further down the arc to the dish so that Jimmy can continue to have success feeding himself.

How could you measure whether you are having any success? In this case it is necessary for the mother to keep track of where she is in the reverse chain feeding process. She might do this by having a chart similar to the following and entering on the chart the date that she mastered the particular skill. This chart would allow her to move in very careful increments to the completion of the reverse chain procedure.

Behavior	Date Mastered
1. Move hand to mouth from dish.	
2. Release hand one inch from mouth.	
3. Release hand three inches from mouth.	
4. Release hand five inches from mouth.	
5. Release hand seven inches from mouth.	
6. Release hand 10 inches from mouth.	
7. Release hand 13 inches from mouth (add any additional step required).	
8. Release hand immediately above plate.	
9. Release hand as food is scooped.	
10. Child scoops food himself.	

Chapter 9

"ISN'T IT TIME HE OUTGREW THIS?"

or

Toilet Training Made Easy

Of all the areas of child training, the most exasperating and difficult one for parents is usually toilet training. Perhaps the reason for this is that any failures in the program are so obvious. It often happens that the entire process of toilet training becomes an unpleasant experience for both parent and child. We have often found that parents can be making real progress with their child, but the unpleasantness of a few dirty diapers hides the fact that the child is going to the bathroom more often. As a result, progress goes unnoticed. Therefore, we cannot stress too heavily the importance of record keeping in toilet training.

This chapter presents an approach with which we have had considerable success in training the child who has not yet learned to go to the bathroom. This chapter places a heavy emphasis upon keeping track of how well you are doing. Record keeping will also enable you to decide when is the right time of day to conduct your training.

PINPOINTING THE BEHAVIOR

If we were to analyze the process of toilet training from a behavioral point of view, we would decide that the difficulty does not lie in the actual behavior. There is nothing wrong with elimination. We do not want to reduce its frequency, increase its frequency or eliminate it entirely. The real problem is in the cue—where the behavior is performed. The learning problem for the child is to recognize the cues that signal to him that the behavior is about to occur so that he may do something appropriate about it. So our actual training could be called training in cue establishment or cue control. We wish to teach our child that this behavior cannot happen anytime and any place.

So essentially our training is:

RIGHT CUES + BEHAVIOR = REINFORCEMENT

WRONG CUES + BEHAVIOR = NO REINFORCEMENT

We want to attach cues to the behavior. We wish for the natural cues of a full pressure upon the bladder to lead the child into the bathroom. Our training is to set up a situation which will maximize the chances of our obtaining the behavior when those cues are present. We want the child in the bathroom and on the toilet when he is ready to urinate.

To do this we must pinpoint the behavior in terms of when it is most likely to occur. Some times are more natural times for going to the bathroom than others; for example, the first thing in the morning. Most children, however, tend to go a certain amount of time after meals or at other fairly regular times during the day. What we would like you to do is to spend the first week of your program simply listing for each day the time of the day your child messed his pants. Of course, sometimes you do not discover the accident until a considerable amount of time after it has occurred. In that case merely make an educated guess as to what time the accident occurred. Keep track of this every day. Below is the kind of record we mean. Then at the end of the week count up the times the behavior occurred and try to determine the most likely times of the day your child will go to the bathroom. It may well be that the number one time is right after he gets up. That may be fol-

	Mon.	Tues.	Wed.	Thurs.	Fri.	Sat.	Sun.
Got up	7:30						
Wet Pants	7:45						
Breakfast	8:00						
Wet Pants	8:50						
Taken to Toilet Nothing Happened	10:00						
Lunch	12:00						
Wet and Messed Pants	1:00						
Played Outside	1:30–3:30						
Taken to Bathroom Nothing Happened	3:40						
Wet Pants	4:15						
Dinner	6:00						
Taken to Bathroom Nothing Happened	6:30						
Wet Pants	7:05						
Taken to Bathroom Nothing Happened	8:00						
Bed	8:20						

lowed by one-half hour or perhaps one hour after meals; then perhaps again late in the evening. This particular child seems to go 50 to 65 minutes after every meal. Once you have established those times they will tell you when you want to do your training. That is, you will know the times your child is most likely to have to go to the bathroom. Your job then is to make sure that he goes to the bathroom and that he performs the behavior when you have set up the right cues.

CUES

There are a number of cues that will eventually be associated with going to the bathroom. The most basic is a natural cue or the feeling of pressure from the bladder. Eventually this will prompt your child to go to the bathroom—alone.

Our approach is to allow the cues of the bathroom, such as the toilet, etc. to become attached to the actual behavior. We do our training at the times you have determined when your child is most likely to have to go to the bathroom. That means we will pick times when there are most likely to be cues to your child from the pressure upon his bladder. You will also have to be there during this part of the training as a reinforcing agent. But as the program moves along, your presence gradually will be removed so that at the end of the training the behavior is under the control of the proper cues. Again, those cues are bladder pressure and the physical surroundings of the bathroom.

Our training procedure in cue control proceeds in the following sequence:

1. Using your chart, select the times your child is most likely to have to go to the bathroom and begin your initial training session at that time.

2. You and your child should proceed together to the toilet. As you go there, ask him, "Do you feel like you have to go to

the bathroom now?" This simply helps him to call attention to his own natural cues.

3. Have your child sit on the toilet and you wait next to him until the behavior occurs. As soon as it does, that will signal you to reinforce him. You should use primarily praise

and encouragement. You should attempt to make this event as important as possible. You may want to call in your husband and discuss the event. In short, you should make this seem like one of the major turning points in world history. Any other reinforcer to be used should also be given now.

4. If nothing occurs, you should wait no longer than five to 10 minutes before terminating the session. We find it is best not to drag out the session until it becomes unpleasant. You should then take a short break remembering that your child probably has to go to the bathroom around this time. If the session is occurring first thing in the morning, you may wish to go to the dining room and have some juice. Once the child has had some more liquid, you should return again to the bathroom and repeat the procedure, again waiting no longer than five to 10 minutes if nothing happens. If you have selected

your time carefully, you should find that eventually the response will occur, enabling you to reinforce it. When your child finally urinates and you have reinforced him, you should record this on the kind of chart we will show you later in the chapter. This record, of course, lets you know how well you are doing; but it also will help to tell you when you are ready to go to the next stage of the program. When your chart tells you that you are getting nearly all the behaviors in the toilet rather than in the pants, you are ready to begin the second stage of the program.

108   *Isn't It Time He Outgrew This?*

5. This sequence of the training is designed to remove you from the training situation and teach the child to be able to go by himself. During this step you should take your child into the bathroom and sit him on the toilet. However, you

should not be standing next to your child ready to reinforce him. You should wait in the bathroom, *not* next to the toilet; but at least a few feet away. When the child finally goes, then again reward him. You may not have to be as enthusiastic as you were the first few times, but nevertheless continue to reinforce him. Then you will have him wash his hands by himself and leave the bathroom.

6. When your chart shows that you have done this procedure two or three times successfully, then you will begin the

next phase. You should take him just to the doorway of the bathroom and let him walk to the toilet himself. You will not wait in the middle of the bathroom but rather wait by the doorway. Again, when he has been successful, you will reinforce him.

7. At this stage you should wait in the doorway or slightly outside the bathroom. Again, you will reinforce him when he is finished. Then he should wash his hands by himself. You should also, at this point, begin waiting a bit longer to reinforce him. He now may be able to finish on the toilet and wash his hands and dry them before you reward him. One of the most effective rewards is telling him that he is a big boy and that

"*Isn't It Time He Outgrew This?*" 111

he is growing up, as all children seem to realize that their older brothers and sisters are toilet trained.

8. At this point you will wish to wait outside of the bathroom, a few feet into the next room. You should take your child to this point and let him go the rest of the way by himself.

He should then sit on the toilet, with the door open and with you still in sight. But you must definitely be in the next room. Again, when he has finished the entire procedure, you should reinforce him.

9. The next step should be with you even farther into the room, perhaps barely visible to him. Again when your chart indicates he is doing this successfully, then you may wish to go on to the next step.

10. At this point your child should be taken to the bathroom and the door closed after him. So he should be alone in the room, but he should know by now that he will be reinforced for repeating the entire procedure. At this stage when your child wishes to go, you should teach him how to let you know by somehow telling you he has to go; and you should only need to point out the bathroom or indicate that he should go. You will no longer need to walk him even close to the bathroom.

Again, it is important to keep track at each stage of how well your child is doing. Once you have gotten the initial steps across to him, each stage in which you remove yourself farther from the bathroom should proceed smoothly. After each stage is done successfully, two or three times, then you should go on to the next stage. However, if your chart indicates that at one particular part you are having difficulty and he is not performing in the bathroom or he is making a puddle on the bathroom floor, then you know that you have proceeded too fast in removing yourself from the situation. You should then back up and go to the previous stage and stay at that level until you have two or three successes again and then return to the next stage. The criteria then for advancing to the next step is that there is no disruption in his performance as you fade yourself out of the bathroom.

REINFORCEMENT

As we indicated in the previous section, the major reinforcement should be your enthusiasm and support of his behavior. This is a big stage in his development and you should let him know how proud you are of his performance. If you feel that something else is needed, then do not hesitate to use any other kind of reinforcement. Tokens can work very well here. You may wish to read the chapter on tokens to indicate how these can best be used. Also, candy is successful. Do not be disturbed by the rather strange sight of popping candy into the mouth of a child who is sitting on the toilet. As long as a reinforcement is effective it should be used. We have, also, had considerable success in making a chart for the child in which a star or some other kind of mark is posted (where everyone can see it) each time he successfully goes to the bathroom. These stars may also function as tokens and when so many are earned he may be able to trade these for a special reinforcement. In many cases, however, just the stars, themselves, will be suitable reinforcement. We feel that by using this procedure and by doing things like posting a public record of his performance that you are telling your child there is nothing unpleasant or dirty or nasty about toilet training. You are indicating to him this is simply another area of training like learning to tie his shoes, and if he has been successful in these areas previously, he should be successful in toilet training.

KEEPING TRACK

There are basically two types or methods of records you will want to keep. The first one is simply a form (like the one

"Isn't It Time He Outgrew This?"

TOILET TRAINING CHART

△ = Bowel Movement in Toilet ◯ = Urination in Toilet
▲ = Bowel Movement ⊗ = Urination
X = Child on Potty; No Results

[Toilet training chart with time slots from 7:00 AM to 8:00 PM in 30-minute intervals along the rows, and days 1 through 15 as columns, filled with the symbols defined above.]

earlier in the chapter) which you use during the first week. By filling out this record, it will tell you when your child goes to the bathroom most often and when your training should be done.

The next record simply indicates the success your child is having on a daily basis. Each day is broken down into half hour periods. The parent records using the two symbols of circles and triangles. A triangle indicates a bowel movement; a circle indicates a urination. If the bowel movement occurs in the toilet, the triangle is placed on the chart with no other marking. If the bowel movement, however, occurs in the diaper, a triangle is placed on the chart with an X within it. The same system is used for urination, a circle on the chart without the X indicates that the urination occurred on the potty; a circle with an X indicates that urination occurred in the diaper; an X on the chart without any other mark indicates that the child was placed on the potty but without result. A count each day of the number of bowel movements and number of urinations which occurred in the toilet as opposed to in the diaper will give a daily record which will tell you not only when you are being successful but when you can begin to make the changes into next stages of the program. The chart on page 115 has been partially filled out to show you what a completed chart looks like.

SPECIAL TECHNIQUES

The previous training procedure assumes that the whole sequence of behaviors such as going to the bathroom and sitting on the toilet have already been established. For some children toilet training has already become unpleasant enough that even entering the bathroom is avoided. Some children have become afraid of the bathroom, the toilet and the whole toilet training experience.

If this is so, then you will simply have to begin your training at an earlier point. You will probably, also, need some other reinforcements like candy or something which your child highly prizes. With the reinforcer you simply reward your child for approaching the bathroom and for doing all those preliminary behaviors which lead up to entering the bathroom. For instance, you may ask your child to get up from where he is playing and walk over close to the bathroom, stopping at the point where he begins to get a little afraid or upset. At that point you reinforce him with the candy or whatever reinforcer you have chosen, and again tell him how big he is for having accomplished this step successfully.

Sometime later, one-half hour to an hour perhaps, you want to repeat the procedure, this time getting a bit closer to the bathroom, and when you have gotten as far as the child seems to want to go without getting upset, then you reinforce him again. This procedure is continued until your child can walk into the bathroom and sit on the toilet by himself. Again, if you are proceeding too fast, your child will tell you by getting upset or by beginning to cry. That behavior should signal you to stop the session and then next time do not require your child to go as far before you reinforce him. Again, the important part is if you are keeping track each day, at least by taking notes, you will know how far along you are and when you are proceeding too fast.

Another major problem tends to be the child who is a bedwetter. Provided this is not a medical problem there are a number of ways of handling it. You will often find that toilet training during the day will carry over into the evening and the bedwetting problems will stop. If not, then the procedure must be to teach your child to get up out of bed when he feels sufficient pressure from the bladder. This type of training is usually the hardest on parents. It requires them getting up every few hours during the night and checking whether or not the child is wet. You should find that you can then pin down the time when the behavior occurs perhaps to a three-hour period. When this is done, you must begin getting up every hour during the three-hour period, so that you can further determine when the behavior is most likely to occur. Once you have pinned this down as closely as you can, then you must get your child up right before you believe the behavior is likely to occur and get him into the bathroom. Your child, at this point, is usually relaxed enough that it does not stir up any kind of a struggle and once he gets into the bathroom he urinates. So the problem is really getting yourself up often during the night so that you can pinpoint the behavior. Once you have been successful in getting your child up and into the bathroom and he has urinated there, then you may wish to be increasingly more gentle as you wake him up at that time. At first you may have to shake him, but as you go along you may find that just simply touching him will signal him to get up and go to the bathroom. If you work gradually enough at it, you should find that he is about to get up or is getting up as you come towards his bed.

We recommend toilet training during the day to begin with and if there is an additional bed-wetting problem ignoring that until the daytime training has been completed. If you find that the daytime training is not helping with the bed-wetting problem at night, you should continue your training then as well.

In bed-wetting, as well as toilet training, our procedure assumes that this is simply a learning problem. If you feel that there are other medical problems or problems such as constipation, etc. you should not hesitate to consult a physician. Our approach assumes that you are teaching a healthy child who is physically capable of doing what you expect him to do. If the problem is more than just a learning or training problem, then medical help is certainly needed.

As a final note as far as special techniques go, you will find that the success of the program boils down to the attitude that is present during the training. It can be a thoroughly unpleasant experience and no one enjoys cleaning up dirty diapers. But punishing your child for a dirty diaper really does not train him to go to the bathroom. For one reason the punishment usually comes sometime after the behavior has occurred, and it is not likely to be effective. Also, considerable research has shown that punishment is effective only when there is an alternative behavior that can be rewarded. Simply punishing your child for messing in his pants will not teach him to go to the bathroom. However, you may find a time that you are forced to bite your lip in order to be pleasant during the training. If you can establish a happy, enjoyable session for your child by your attitude and by keeping the session short, and if you can make your child feel that he is accomplishing a tremendous objective, you will find the toilet training procedure much faster and much easier.

EXAMPLE 1

Your first foster child, Rodney, age four, came to live at your house today. Shortly after lunch you notice that he began tugging at the front of his pants. When you asked if he had to go to the bathroom, he said "no." A few minutes later he was crossing his legs. When you asked again, you got the same answer.

Deciding that something needed to be done you took him by the hand. However, as soon as he saw the bathroom, he dropped to the floor, started shrieking and refused to go any further.

When the shock wore off, your years of experience as a mother told you that what you saw in Rodney's face was pure fright. What do you do?

Answer: Whatever has been Rodney's experience in toilet training certainly has not been pleasant. Your best approach is to select something you know is a strong reinforcer to Rodney—something immediate like candy.

Explain to Rodney that this is a game and let us see how many steps he can take (toward the bathroom). Reinforce him after the first step or two. Then reinforce him as soon as you can see him tense up *after* a step. Go as far as your judgment thinks is reasonable. You may not make the bathroom the first time. Make a note of how far you got. The next time begin a few steps behind that point and try again. Make sure he goes farther this time. Continue these sessions until he is in the bathroom. Afterward, reinforce him only for entering the bathroom, sitting down and during your actual toilet training.

EXAMPLE 2

Raymond, a moderately retarded boy of eight was constantly messing his pants. No amount of training seemed to work. His attitude about it was quite healthy. In fact, he would tell you whenever he had just messed.

Whenever this happened his mother would yank off his clothes and whisk him into the shower, where he would frolic in the water, all the while giggling about it. What do you do?

Answer: You should consider whether Raymond does not find the shower so much fun that he messes his pants to get into it. (This was the case with a child we worked with several years ago.) If so, then try to switch things around. Tell Raymond that you will check him in one hour, and if his pants are clean he can take a shower. If not, then you can change his clothes, but no shower. It may even be all right to let him wear his dirty pants for a while. However, he showers only when you find his pants clean. Once he starts coming around, you should check every 1½ to 2 hours, and work toward one check and one shower a day.

Chapter 10

ZIP YOUR ZIPPER

LIKE A GOOD BOY!

or

How to Teach Your Child to Dress Himself

DRESSING SKILLS ARE not usually listed by parents as an area of maximum concern. There seem to be two reasons for this. First, there are a variety of other behaviors in which the child has deficits that are of more concern to the parent; therefore, being able to dress oneself is not very high on the priority list. Second, it is much easier and more efficient if the parent dresses the child herself. To allow the child to dress himself without assistance usually means that a lot of time is involved and that you will be late for wherever it is that you are going.

Dressing skills themselves require a variety of motor skills and you may find reference to the development of these behaviors in the chapter on motor skills. Most parents have found that if they continue to dress the child for a long enough period of time he will eventually be able to do much of the dressing himself. We are suggesting that learning to dress oneself is no different than any other task that has to be learned and can be subjected to similar training techniques.

One of the reasons that children learn to dress themselves after a long period of help by the parent is that they have rehearsed the individual steps many, many times and gradually take the responsibility for completing the steps by themselves. Given this eventual outcome we suggest that you utilize parts of this procedure in a systematic way. You should continue to help the child dress himself except for the last few steps which you let the child finish by himself. Once he is able to accomplish this task, then you should help him through the first part of the dressing sequence and allow him to have more of the task to complete. This whole concept is called reverse chaining and it suggests that you should teach the child from the end to the beginning. That is to say, you should first teach the terminal behaviors, or those that come at the end of the task, such as pulling the pants up the last three inches.

PINPOINTING AND ANALYZING THE BEHAVIOR

In order to be able to successfully plan an attack on this problem you must again start with pinpointing the desired behaviors you wish to teach. This suggests that you should take a complex dressing task and break it down into a number of steps. Try it on yourself and see how many individual steps you think are required to put on a T-shirt. Once you have pinpointed each of the steps, you have basically sequenced your program. Write this sequence down and use it as a guideline for teaching your child. See the illustrations for an example of the sequence. If the first step in the sequence is to unfold the T-shirt independently, then this will become the last thing that we try to teach the child. If the last thing in the sequence is being able to tuck the shirt in, then this will become the

Zip Your Zipper, Like a Good Boy! 123

Child unfolds and puts on T-shirt.

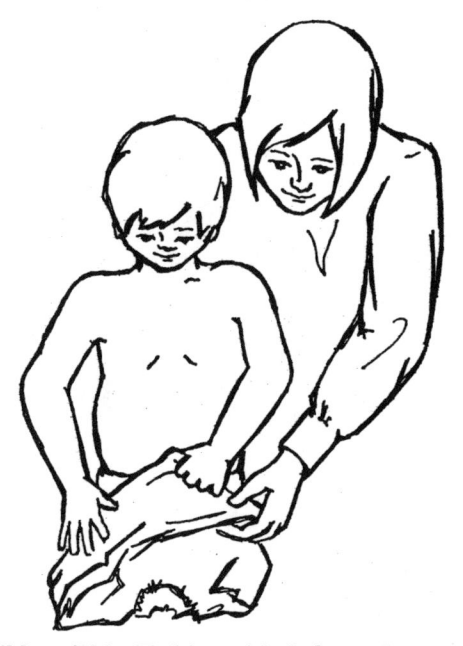

Child unfolds T-shirt with help and puts on.

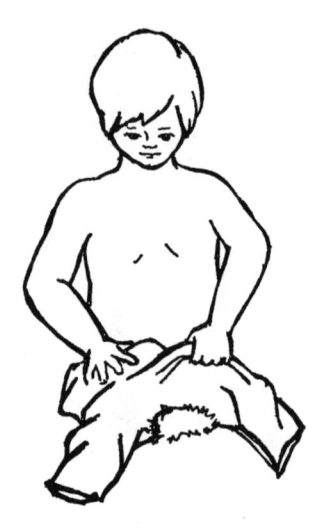

Child puts on T-shirt when placed in lap.

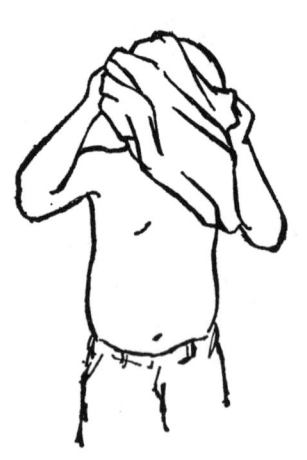

Child puts on T-shirt when placed on head.

Zip Your Zipper, Like a Good Boy! 125

Child puts on T-shirt when placed over his head.

Child puts on T-shirt when over head, one hand to sleeve opening.

Isn't It Time He Outgrew This?

Child puts on T-shirt when one arm through sleeve.

Child puts on T-shirt when one arm through, other hand to opening.

Child puts on T-shirt when one arm through, other half-way in.

Child puts on T-shirt when both arms through sleeves.

first thing that we teach. The following is an example of another sequence of putting on pants.

7. Child unfolds pants and puts on.
6. Child puts on pants when placed in front of him.
5. Child puts on pants when one foot started in.
4. Child puts on pants when one foot in and other started in.
3. Child puts on pants when both feet in (to ankles).
2. Child puts on pants when pulled to knees.
1. Child puts on pants when pulled to thighs.

CUES

When analyzing your training program, you should again revert back to examining the various cues that you are going to provide that will tell the child what behavior is expected of him. In teaching of dressing skills probably the best rule of thumb that can be utilized is, in the beginning, always to use oversize materials, therefore exaggerating the cues you are giving the child. If you are going to teach the child to put on his stockings or his T-shirt, use an extra large size—one of his brother's or his dad's. This will allow him to easily manipulate the material and have success in completing the task. As he increases his proficiency with these oversize materials, you can gradually reduce the size of the clothing that you give him until he can accomplish the same task with his own size.

REINFORCEMENT

In most cases the reinforcement that is available for the child is the completion of the task. If you have helped him through the first section of the task, in allowing him to complete the task then the reinforcement becomes the fact that he has finished it and now he is dressed. The other aspect of reinforcement that comes into play is that a child is always moving toward an area that is known to him and that he has been successful with in the past. For example, as you add new behaviors for him to learn, such as in the case of the stockings, he is always moving towards completion of the task with which he has already had success and that is pulling the stocking up the last three or four inches. He can also see the completed task; if this is paired with your enthusiasm and excitement for his success, that is often quite sufficient amount of reinforcement. However, if you are having difficulties, do not hesitate to use whatever reinforcements are powerful with the child.

SPECIAL TECHNIQUES

If you take a task such as putting on a pair of stockings, you should use oversize stockings and you should help him put the stocking on all the way over the heel and then let him pull it up the last three or four inches. Once he can do this reliably, then you help him put the stocking on just to the heel and let him complete the task. After this is accomplished, you help him put the stocking on to just below the heel and let him complete the task and systematically keep reducing your support and cues until he can put his foot in the stocking and pull it on all the way by himself. This same procedure should be utilized for putting on pants, shirts and other pieces of apparel. In essence, what you are doing is *helping him with the begin-*

ning of the task and making him complete more and more of the task as he becomes proficient. You should also be using oversize material and gradually reducing the size of the material as he demonstrates accomplishment at the various stages.

For things like buttoning that require a great deal of fine motor coordination, you should very definitely go to oversize buttons sewn on a piece of cloth that can be used for practice. For this activity you should use the same reverse chaining procedures. Put the button through the hole nearly all the way and let the child pull it through the last quarter inch for completion. He has now finished the task and had success. Next, push the button only halfway through the hole and let him complete the task, then only a fourth of the way and so on until he can do the whole sequence by himself.

We should be as careful as possible in selecting clothing for the child to wear to insure that he can have maximum success in dressing himself. For example, very early in life you may want to avoid clothing that has very small buttons and fit very tightly as these will be most difficult for him to master. There are dolls that are made with buttons and zippers that are sufficiently oversize so that the child can practice these activities.

In the case of shoes, it may be your decision not to use shoes that require tying until you have practiced the fine motor skills necessary to accomplish shoe tying. Elsewhere in this book the principles of tying shoes using the "rabbit ear" method as described should be utilized for initial training (see Chap. 2). It should also be noted you should never try to teach a child to tie a shoe using a standard shoe and a very small shoelace. It is much more efficient to use one of the dad's very large tennis shoes and a very large shoestring that is easy for the child to grasp. You may even wish to exaggerate these cues even further by first teaching the child to tie the appropriate knot utilizing a very small rope.

Another procedure for providing the child with maximum cues is to use color codes. For example, in the case of tying shoelaces you may find it is helpful during practice to color half the shoelace red and the other half white to allow the child to examine more closely what is required in tying a knot. Another example would be to paint a color on the sole of the right shoe and train him that color goes on the right foot. It has even been suggested to go as far as painting the right big toenail red and putting a red dot on the right shoe sole.

SUMMARY

There are some key things that you must remember when approaching the problem of teaching dressing skills.

You as the parent must be willing to spend the extra time to allow the child to partially dress himself.

You must also make a serious attempt at defining the various steps that are required to accomplish the particular dressing task. Once you have defined these steps you should write them down and use them as your guide in training. If you find that the child cannot easily move from step 4 to step 5, then your first assumption should be that it is too large a step and perhaps there should be a step 4½.

You should try to teach whenever possible from the end to the beginning, that is, helping the child all the way through the task and letting him complete it. If he achieves success, give him more and more responsibility, but you always initiate the first few steps until the very end.

Utilize oversize materials and gradually reduce them in size until he can handle his own clothing. Avoid trying to engage the child in behaviors that require very fine motor activity until he has practiced these skills with oversize materials.

Make the cues as obvious as possible and always allow him to complete the task with maximum reinforcement.

The following are some examples of dressing sequences.

EXAMPLES OF DRESSING PROGRAMS

A. Remove Pants
  5. Child removes pants.
  4. Child removes pants when pulled to thighs.
  3. Chile removes pants when pulled to knees.
  2. Child removes pants when pulled to ankles.
  1. Child removes pants when one leg removed.

B. Put on pants
  7. Child unfolds pants and puts on.
  6. Child puts on pants when placed in front of him.
  5. Child puts on pants when one foot started in.
  4. Child puts on pants when one foot in and other started in.
  3. Child puts on pants when both feet in (to ankles).
  2. Child puts on pants when pulled to knees.
  1. Child puts on pants when pulled to thighs.

C. Remove T-shirt
  6. Child removes T-shirt.

Zip Your Zipper, Like a Good Boy!

   5. Child removes T-shirt when both arms in sleeves, pulled up to shoulder.
   4. Child removes T-shirt when left arm in, right half in.
   3. Child removes T-shirt when left arm in, right arm out.
   2. Child removes T-shirt when left arm half in.
   1. Child removes T-shirt when around neck.
D. Put on T-shirt
   10. Child unfolds and puts on T-shirt.
   9. Child puts on T-shirt with help and puts on.
   8. Child puts on T-shirt when placed in lap.
   7. Child puts on T-shirt when placed on head.
   6. Child puts on T-shirt when placed over his head.
   5. Child puts on T-shirt when over head, one hand to sleeve opening.
   4. Child puts on T-shirt when one lower arm through sleeve.
   3. Child puts on T-shirt when one arm through, other hand to opening.
   2. Child puts on T-shirt when one arm through, other half-way in.
   1. Child puts on T-shirt when both arms through sleeves.
E. Remove sock
   4. Child removes sock.
   3. Child removes sock when just above heel.
   2. Child removes sock when just below heel.
   1. Child removes sock from toes.
F. Put on sock
   5. Child puts on sock (heel in correct position).
   4. Child puts on sock when handed to him with heel in correct position.
   3. Child puts on sock when toes started in.
   2. Child puts on sock when just below heel.
   1. Child puts on sock when just above heel.
G. Remove shoe
   4. Child removes shoe (laces loosened).

3. Child removes shoe when heel slipped half way out.
2. Child removes shoe when heel slipped all the way out.
1. Child removes shoe when shoe half off.

H. Put on shoe
6. Child puts a shoe on the correct foot when available to him.
5. Child puts a shoe on the correct foot when shoes placed in front of his feet.
4. Child puts on a shoe when toes in opening.
3. Child puts on a shoe when toes half way in.
2. Child puts on shoe with heel out.
1. Child puts on shoe when heel just started in.

I. Remove jacket
5. Child removes jacket.
4. Child removes jacket when pulled off shoulders.
3. Child removes jacket with one arm in, one half in.
2. Child removes jacket with one arm in.
1. Child removes jacket with one arm half in.

J. Put on jacket
8. Child puts on jacket when positioned beside him.
7. Child puts on jacket when guided to hold right side.
6. Child puts on jacket when right hand started in sleeve.
5. Child puts on jacket when right arm half way in sleeve.
4. Child puts on jacket when right arm in sleeve.
3. Child puts on jacket when right side on shoulder, left hand in sleeve.
2. Child puts on jacket when right side on shoulder, left arm in below elbow.
1. Child puts on jacket when right side on shoulder, left arm in above elbow.

CASE HISTORY I

Mrs. Jones approaches Johnny's preschool teacher with the following complaint:

"I just cannot seem to get Johnny to dress himself completely. I have to help him with so many parts of his cloth-

Zip Your Zipper, Like a Good Boy!

ing. I really do not think that your techniques of reverse chaining, having him dress by one step at a time, is working."

As the preschool teacher, you look at Johnny and the way he is dressed and you note that he is wearing overalls with straps and bottoms, high top lace shoes and form fitting long-sleeved turtle necked shirts.

What is your recommendation to Mrs. Jones?

Case History I—Answer

You should probably suggest to Mrs. Jones that the clothes which Johnny is wearing do not facilitate his learning to dress himself. It would be better if he were wearing pants with elastic waist, loafers or elastic binding shoes without laces to begin with, or at the very least low top shoes with laces, and looser fitting shirts, around the neck and short sleeved if possible. If long sleeve shirts are required, find shirts that are looser fitting in general.

Once Mrs. Jones has made these modifications in clothing, then commence a detailed program with her, having her go through the reverse chain procedure.

CASE HISTORY II

Mrs. Smith is ready to begin to teach Timothy to dress himself. Timothy already knows how to undress himself. He can take off all his clothes, but has not yet learned to put any of the articles back on. Mrs. Smith decides that the first article of clothing that she is going to teach Timothy to put on by himself is his socks. Timothy normally wears, short, white ankle-height socks.

Mrs. Smith has carefully read this book and deduces that she is going to use the reverse chain procedure for putting on socks. She successfully moves through all of the steps one at a time and finally reaches the last step. The last step is for Timothy to take the sock and place it over his toes and pull it up over his heel and up to the correct position on his leg.

Timothy seems unable to accomplish this. The sock gets

caught in his toes. He manifests behavior which Mrs. Smith interprets as frustration, throws the sock down and says, "I can't do it." Mrs. Smith hands him the sock again and he tries again, but with the same results. What would you suggest to Mrs. Smith?

Case History II—Answer

Mrs. Smith has successfully gone through the reverse chain procedure with the exception of one last step and that is placing on the sock. Notice that the sock is getting caught in the toes and that the child apparently is having difficulty opening the hole of the sock and getting it over his toes so that he can then pull it up. He has already demonstrated that once over his toes, he is capable of pulling it up. Thus, we must teach the child to put the sock over his toes. It is suggested that the best way to do this is to give the child an oversized sock to practice on and then gradually closing the hole of the sock as he places it over his toes. This can be done by taking a couple of stitches in the head of the sock or by gradually reducing the size of socks used. If he achieves this success with a large size sock, and we move to lesser size socks, we can gradually shape his behavior down to his normal sock and let him continue to dress himself.

CASE HISTORY III

Mrs. Brown is teaching Sammy to put on his pants using the reverse chain procedures. Sammy has successfully gone through the first step in the reverse chain procedure, pulling up his pants from his hips, the second step, pulling them up from his thighs, and the third step, pulling them up from his knees. When he gets to the fourth step of pulling the pants up from his ankles, his knees seem to get in the way and he is having all sorts of difficulties. What suggestions would you make for Mrs. Brown?

Case History III—Answer

The first thing that Mrs. Brown should do is to look at the sequence of her reverse chain procedure. Perhaps with Sammy the step is too big between the knees and the ankles. Sammy has demonstrated that he can pull his pants up from the knees. He is having difficulty pulling them up from the ankles. Therefore, Mrs. Brown should make the next step somewhere between the knees and the ankles and preferably just below the knees. It may be necessary to have a step just below the knees and then another a few inches below that before Mrs. Brown resumes the regular sequence of having Sammy pull his pants up from the ankles.

Chapter 11

"WASH YOUR HANDS BEFORE YOU EAT"

or

How to Teach Hygiene Skills

A VISITOR TO our country need only spend one evening before a television set to learn that we are a nation devoted to cleanliness. Commercial after commercial exhorts us "to use Dinko soap so that we will not offend when we are close to other people even at the end of a long day," "to brush our teeth with Smilo toothpaste for pleasant breath odor and whiter teeth," and "to use Groomey for our hair for that soft natural look that will make women want to run their fingers through our tresses." An inexhaustible series of commercials tell us to be clean, to smell good and to use the proper combination of soap, cream, liquid, deodorant and paste to make our appearance pleasing to the rest of the world.

The visitor to our country will have this impression of a nation devoted to cleanliness reinforced if he is able to spend a day in the home of an "average" American family. There, he will hear mother in the morning after breakfast reminding her children, "Don't forget to brush your teeth," and inspecting Charlie as he goes out the door and turning him around to the bathroom and saying "Go brush your hair before you go to school." And so it goes throughout the day until the evening meal. Rare is the child in our culture who is able to move to the table without the motherly dictum of "Wash your hands before you eat."

And so, it is only natural that we who are writing for parents should devote some attention to techniques for teaching the handicapped child hygiene habits, for they hold an established place in our culture. This chapter, therefore, is devoted to discussing some techniques for teaching handicapped children hygiene habits. We have chosen three which we think are representative of the many you will have to instruct—washing of hands, brushing of teeth, and combing of hair. The techniques which we shall show you for washing of hands can be extended to washing of face and taking of baths. Techniques for combing one's hair can be used for teaching a child to brush his hair or brush his clothes.

WASHING HANDS

Pinpointing the Behavior

Washing of hands is a complex behavior which consists of a series of simple behaviors. Even children who are not handicapped need this task broken down for them in very definite steps so that in completing the overall complex behavior of washing hands, they will complete all of the simple behaviors of washing the back of hands, washing the front of hands, washing fingers, and so on, until they can pass the inevitable inspection before they eat. The following shows an analysis of the complex behavior, washing of hands.

1. Child turns on cold water.
2. Child turns on hot water so as to achieve warm water with which to wash hands.
3. Child removes soap from soap dish.
4. Child holds soap between both hands and places both hands and soap beneath the running water.
5. Child rubs both hands with soap.
6. Child places soap either back in soap dish or on side of sink.
7. Child rubs both hands together working up lather with soap.
8. Child takes right hand and rubs soapy lather on back of left hand.
9. Child rubs soapy lather with right hand around little finger of left hand.

10. Child rubs soapy lather with right hand around fourth finger of left hand.
11. Child rubs soapy lather with right hand around middle finger of left hand.
12. Child rubs soapy lather with right hand around index finger of left hand.
13. Child rubs soapy lather with right hand around thumb of left hand.
14. Child picks up soap.
15. Child places both hands and soap beneath faucet.
16. Child takes hands out from beneath faucet and rubs soap together with both hands.
17. Child replaces soap on soap dish or side of sink.
18. Child uses left hand to rub back of right hand.
19. Child rubs soapy lather with left hand around little finger of right hand.
20. Child rubs soapy lather with left hand around fourth finger of right hand.
21. Child rubs soapy lather with left hand around middle finger of right hand.
22. Child rubs soapy lather with left hand around index finger of right hand.
23. Child rubs soapy lather with left hand around thumb of right hand.
24. Child rinses hands under water.
25. Child shuts off hot water.
26. Child shuts off cold water.

Thus, one can see that washing of hands, broken down into 26 steps, will require a good deal of teaching of the handicapped child.

Cues

Verbal cues, of course, are absolutely mandatory in hygiene habits. Hopefully, the child will learn to respond to the phrase "Wash your hands." Upon hearing it, he will be able to move independently into the bathroom, go to the sink, and go through the process of washing his hands as outlined above. The phrase, "Wash your hands," in this case may imply, however, drying the hands, although when first teaching the child it may be necessary to instruct him to wash his hands and after he completes that process, then instruct him separately to dry his hands.

Initially, the verbal cue, "Wash your hands," should be coupled with leading the child into the bathroom and starting the hand washing proceudre. Verbal cues may be necessary for each step of the hand washing procedure. For instance, it may be necessary to tell the child, "Turn on the cold water," and point to the correct faucet. It may be then necessary to tell him to "Turn on the hot water," and point to the correct faucet. Each subsequent step, "Get the soap," "Put your hands and the soap under the water," should all initially be verbalized which will mean an entire chain of cues in order to bring together the entire chain of behaviors.

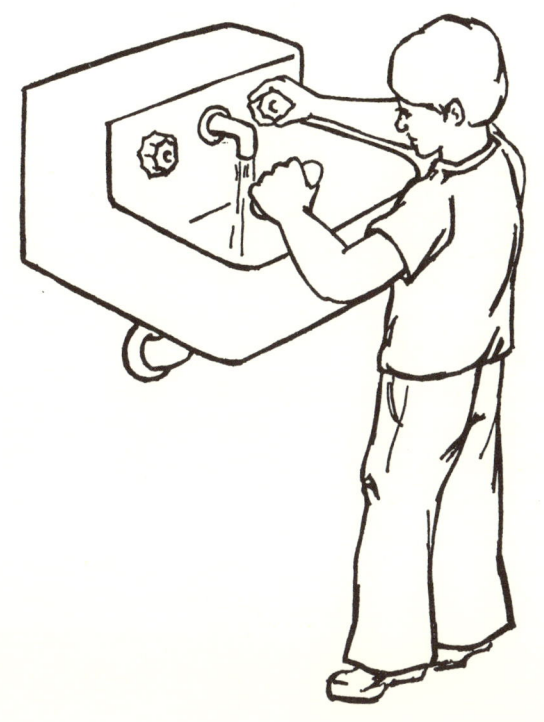

In the case of hand washing, demonstration and moving the child's hands through the motions will be definitely necessary. However, each time that this happens, the appropriate verbal cues should be given and the movement from one step to another should be done slowly and distinctly so that the child sees the relationship from the verbal cue to the movement required.

Another very effective cue for the child is for the parent to wash his hands at the same time as the child. This model for the child's performance can be done in conjunction with the cues mentioned above.

Reinforcement

As we shall mention under special techniques, we recommend that this as well as most other hygiene tasks be taught using a reverse chain procedure. This means as far as reinforcement is concerned that the reinforcement will be administered at the same point in the hand washing procedure, which is after the last step in the sequence, namely shutting off the cold water.

Once again the rule is to choose a reinforcement which has the most meaning for the child. If you have found cereal bits or M&M candies or some other food especially helpful in teaching the child, do not hesitate to use it here. Remember, however, that with the food must also come social praise—hugging, squeezing and verbal praise. "I like the way you are washing your hands, Johnny" or something of this nature. It is always well when administering verbal praise to praise the specific task rather than just "A good boy" or "You're doing a nice job." It is better to say "I like the way you are washing your hands" or "You certainly are washing your hands well" or "I like the way you dry your hands."

One of the difficulties with dispensing the reinforcements in a task like handwashing is the necessity to be ready to give the reinforcement when the task is over, because at that point both mother's and child's hands are soaking wet. (Despite the fact that M&M may melt in your mouth, they also melt in your hand if the hand is wet.) The best and easiest technique has been for the parent usually to help the child wash his hands, keeping a towel very handy so that as soon as the cold water is shut off the parent can quickly dry one hand and pop the goodie into the mouth of the child.

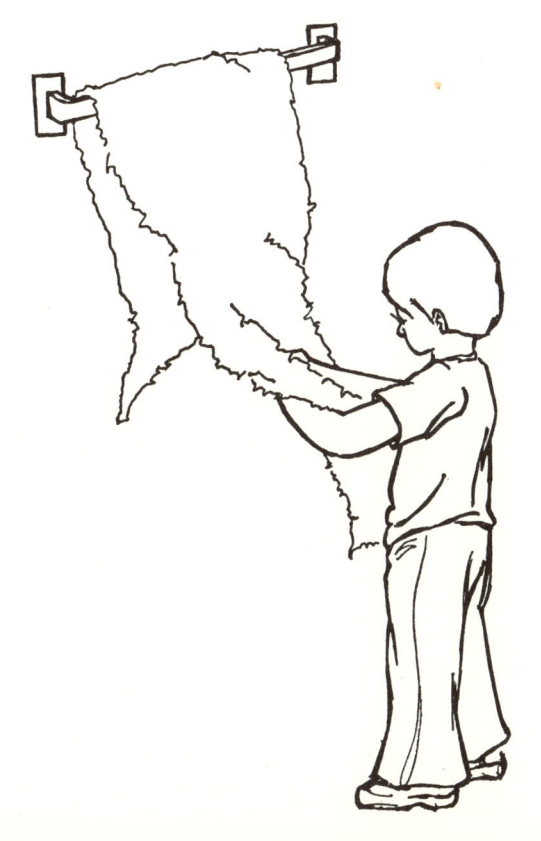

One of the cautions here is that you should not postpone delivering the primary reinforcement if you are going to use such a reinforcement. Remember that one of the things that we do know about reinforcement is that it should be given as soon as possible after the act is completed. And so it would not be wise to wait until you dry the child's hands and lead him from the bathroom into the kitchen to give him the goodie. The goodie should be ready and available and waiting in the bathroom for dispensing to the child as soon as he has shut off that cold water.

Special Techniques

Washing hands like most other motor skills should probably be accomplished using a reverse chain procedure, which means that you would do step 1 through 25 with the child guiding his hands, helping him go through each and every one of them, providing him the verbal cues at each and every level and then when you reach the last step, 26, to shut off the cold water, you then teach him to do that by himself. That is the first step he would be taught. As soon as the cold water is shut off he is reinforced. Once he has mastered shutting off the cold water without any help, you back up and you teach him step 25 in combination with step 26. He learns to shut off the hot water and then the cold water. When he has mastered those two tasks you chain the last three steps together. You teach the child to rinse his hands, shut off the hot water and then shut off the cold water, always reinforcing him after he shuts off the cold water.

There is only one other thing to be concerned about in the hand-washing task. Can the child reach all the parts of the sink easily? He may need a rather large stool on which to stand so as to be able to reach the soap dish and the two faucets and place his hands easily under the water.

Keeping Track

As with most other self-help skills, usually more than one person will be teaching the child. It is imperative that all members of the family who may be teaching the child the self-help skill allow the child to progress on his own at the point in the teaching process that he is capable of doing so. For instance, little learning would be occurring if when the mother taught the child to wash his hands she was at step 24 allowing him to rinse his hands by himself, yet when father taught him to wash his hands he only allowed him to do step 26 by himself. This would be a very confusing situation for the child as well as restricting the learning process. Therefore, some type of record posted with scotch tape near the bathroom sink will be necessary. We suggest a record of this type: List the 26 steps for washing of hands, place in front of them a blank space as illustrated below. (Only the top portion of the record is shown.) This blank space is to record either checkmark or a date as to when the child successfully accomplished that task. Notice that we have taken the sequence shown previously and reversed it so that the parent knows that the last step is the first step to be taught and is the one shown on the top of the page. The chart shown below has been partially filled out indicating that the child has already mastered steps 26, 25, and 24. He is now on step 23.

X 26. Child shuts off cold water.
X 25. Child shuts off hot water.
X 24. Child rinses hands under water.
  23. Child rubs soapy lather with left hand around thumb of right hand.
  22. Child rubs soapy lather with left hand around index finger of right hand.
  21. Child rubs soapy lather with left hand around middle finger of right hand.
  20. Child rubs soapy lather with left hand around fourth finger of right hand.

Some parents may wish to note the date when the child accomplishes a task. There is one advantage in adding the date. This is sometimes very encouraging to the parent as he sees the rapid progress which the child makes from step to step. Although the task of teaching a child to wash his hands may take many weeks, the movement from step to step may take only a few days each. Sometimes we are overwhelmed by the number of steps which must be taught in such a complex behavior as washing hands. Consequently we as parents can be encouraged if we find that each step is being learned at a fairly rapid rate.

BRUSHING YOUR TEETH

Pinpointing Behavior

Like washing of hands, brushing of teeth is a complex behavior. In fact, we have found that among parents and among families there are definitely different ways of brushing teeth. One of the basic disagreements seems to be as to how you rinse your mouth after completing the task of brushing your teeth. One school of thought maintains that a glass of water should be used and people should rinse their mouth by taking a drink from the glass of water. Another school of thought, equally vocal and militant about their position, maintains that that step is not necessary, but that one can adequately rinse their mouth by rinsing their tooth brush off with water and rinsing their mouth in that manner. We refuse to take sides in this dispute, for as we perceive it, this dispute has all the emotional earmarks of the age-long dispute as to whether or not the tube of toothpaste should be rolled from the bottom or squeezed indiscriminately.

In the interest of neutrality therefore, we have provided two analyses of toothbrushing behavior: The first shows toothbrushing behavior, utilizing a glass of water. The second shows toothbrushing behavior rinsing the mouth by means of wetting the toothbrush.

1. Child turns on cold water.
2. Child places tube of toothpaste in nondominant hand.
3. Child unscrews cap of toothpaste.
4. Child places cap of toothpaste on sink.
5. Child picks up toothbrush.
6. Child wets toothbrush.
7. Child squeezes toothpaste on toothbrush.
8. Child places toothpaste on sink.
9. Child brushes up and down on front portion of teeth.
10. Child brushes up and down on left portion of teeth.
11. Child brushes up and down on right portion of teeth.
12. Child brushes top of lower left teeth.
13. Child brushes top of lower right teeth.
14. Child brushes bottom of upper left teeth.
15. Child brushes bottom of upper right teeth.
16. Child brushes behind lower teeth.
17. Child brushes behind upper teeth.
18. Child rinses toothbrush.
19. Child returns toothbrush to holder.
20. Child picks up glass.

21. Child fills glass with water.
22. Child drinks from glass.
23. Child rinses mouth with water.
24. Child spits out water.
25. Child pours out remaining water from glass.
26. Child returns glass to holder.
27. Child picks up toothpaste with nondominant hand.
28. Child screws on cap of toothpaste.
29. Child returns toothpaste to proper location.

1. Child turns on cold water.
2. Child places tube of toothpaste in nondominant hand.
3. Child unscrews cap of toothpaste.
4. Child places cap of toothpaste on sink.
5. Child picks up toothbrush.
6. Child wets toothbrush.
7. Child squeezes toothpaste on toothbrush.
8. Child places toothpaste on sink.
9. Child brushes up and down on front portion of teeth.
10. Child brushes up and down on left portion of teeth.
11. Child brushes up and down on right portion of teeth.
12. Child brushes top of lower left teeth.
13. Child brushes top of lower right teeth.
14. Child brushes bottom of upper left teeth.
15. Child brushes bottom of upper right teeth.
16. Child brushes behind lower teeth.
17. Child brushes behind upper teeth.
18. Child rinses toothbrush.
19. Child places wet toothbrush in mouth.
20. Child brushes all area of teeth with wet toothbrush.
21. Child rinses toothbrush.
22. Child puts toothbrush away.
23. Child picks up toothpaste with nondominant hand.
24. Child picks up cap with dominant hand.
25. Child screws on cap of toothpaste.
26. Child returns toothpaste to proper location.

Special Techniques

In the case of toothbrushing, the utilization of an electric toothbrush may simplify the entire sequence of teaching the child to make the proper motions manually. Since the electric toothbrush is designed to vibrate rapidly over the teeth and thus clean them, it substitutes for the movement of the hand up and down. An electric toothbrush is strongly recommended for handicapped children. Parents will find that the child can be taught to place the brush in the proper place in the teeth and the electrical motion of the brush will do the rest of the work.

COMBING HAIR

Analyzing Behavior

When one approaches the task of analyzing the behavior of combing a person's hair, one can quickly understand that the steps in combing hair will be as many and as varied as the number of hair styles existing today. To simplify our example let us imagine a young boy who is wearing his hair parted on the left side and generally combed forward so that the bulk of the hair on the right side forms almost a bang-like effect on the forehead. His hair is relatively short. Steps for combing his hair might be as follows:

1. Comb all hair forward. (This may require a number of strokes of the comb as would be true for any of the subsequent steps.)
2. Mark place where part is to be made.
3. Comb hair to the left of the part (many strokes).
4. Comb hair to the right of the part (many strokes).
5. Comb hair to the rear on back of head (many strokes).

Special Techniques

In teaching a child to use a comb, one might utilize some of the same principles in teaching a child to eat—that is, use a large comb, so that he has no difficulty grasping it and manipulating it.

Remember also, that when first teaching the child, one must be willing to accept less than perfection. The part may not be too straight and some spots which should have been combed may have been missed, but initially we should accept these and reinforce the child for his good performance.

CASE HISTORY I

You are a parent of a three-year-old mentally retarded child. You have taught him to wash his own hands and you now desire to teach him to bathe himself. What is the first thing you must do?

Case History I—Answer

The first thing you must do is analyze the behavior of bathing. You must break kown all of the steps required in the sequence of bathing and then make a determination as to whether or not you will teach these in a forward or a reverse chain manner. A reverse chain procedure is recommended.

CASE HISTORY II

You are teaching a child to brush his teeth. In your sequence for teethbrushing you have included using a glass to rinse the child's mouth. The child seems to be having difficulty with this stage and you notice that because his hands are wet the glass tends to slip from his grip and there is danger that he will drop it. What action might you take to remediate this situation?

Case History II—Answer

There are a number of possibilities here. First, one might eliminate the rinsing of the mouth with a glass and use a toothbrush to rinse the mouth. This is a very acceptable procedure and might simplify the entire toothbrushing sequence.

However, if one desires to retain the glass, one might first insure that the glass utilized is plastic and has a rubber edge. Or one might tape some adhesive tape around the glass which would help the child to grasp the glass and not have it slip from his hands.

CASE HISTORY III

You are teaching your child to wash his hands. You have reached a step in the sequence where he is to grasp the soap in his right hand and is to wash the back of his left hand. He does not seem to be able to do this. Or he does not want to do this. You carefully look at the sequence of steps you have organized, but you cannot break these behaviors down any further. What should you do at this point?

Case History III—Answer

First thing to do is to examine the reinforcement that you are using with the child. Are they the strongest reinforcements that you can use? Is there something that he likes above everything else with which you could reward him at the conclusion of the handwashing activity? If so, use that. Then try the sequence again. If you are still having trouble, you might try guiding the child's hands slowly through the motions, and then gradually as days pass provide him less and less guidance with your hands. Continue to use the most powerful reinforcements you can muster for this particular task as you do this guidance, however.

CASE HISTORY IV

You have decided to teach your child to wash his hands. However, he rebels and throws a temper tantrum as soon as you take him over to the sink. What should you do?

Case History IV—Answer

Remember in the chapter on behavior problems you were told that the best thing to do with temper tantrums was to ignore them. As soon as the child ceases the tantrum, however, you should pick him up and say "Johnny I'm glad you've now stopped your crying. I like the way you're being quiet now. Now let us wash our hands." This may have to be repeated a number of times, but the child must have it impressed upon him that he is not going to be able to avoid the handwashing task by means of a temper tantrum.

Chapter 12

Silence Is Not Always Golden

or

"HOW DO WE GET HIM TO TALK"

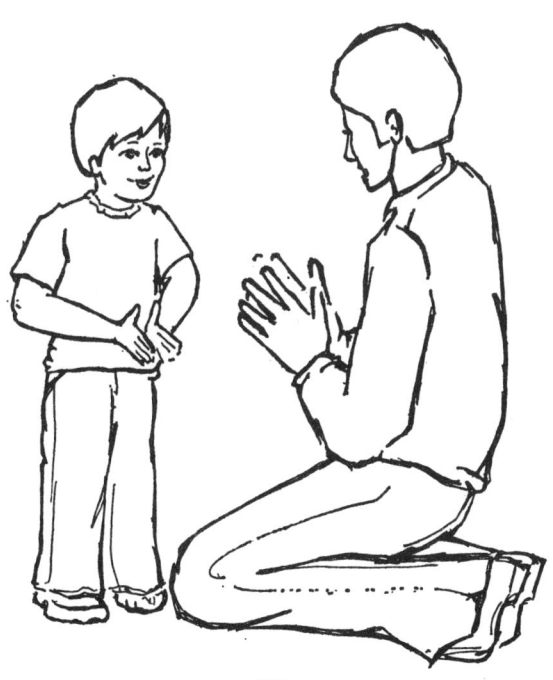

U<small>SE OF LANGUAGE</small> is probably one of the most important tasks that a child has to learn. As a child grows and develops, he typically expands the number of environments to which he is exposed. Our society is verbally oriented and as the child broadens his scope of experiences there will be more and more demands placed upon him to be able to utilize properly his language skills. Anybody with a deficit in language is readily noticeable in our society. Adequate use of language allows the child to express his needs, wishes and desires and to make demands on his environment that are readily understood by others.

In this chapter we will deal with two major aspects of communication, expressive language and receptive language. When we speak of receptive language, we are typically talking about the child's ability to understand what is said to him. Expressive language, on the other hand, deals with the child's ability to verbally communicate with other persons. We feel that the area of language can be most efficiently dealt with if it is divided into these two categories.

RECEPTIVE LANGUAGE

Typically when we talk about somebody who has a language disorder we are referring to somebody who cannot speak clearly. This is far too narrow an interpretation of language problems. The area of receptive language is extremely important as it refers to the child's ability to respond to cues from his environment. For the most part these cues will be of a verbal nature and if you would look closely at the number of verbal cues that you respond to in an hour's time, I'm sure it would amaze you. The overall position taken in this book would support the notion that the ability to follow instructions, respond

PINPOINTING AND ANALYZING BEHAVIOR

Time after time we see people teaching children or giving them a series of instructions only to be frustrated that the child does not adequately respond. When this happens, many people are quick to say that that child is retarded. A better analysis of the situation would be that that child did not understand the instructions that were given and therefore must be taught. It would be very difficult for any of you to respond to the instructions written in this book if they were written in French. This is not to say that you could not learn to respond to French instructions; it only says that you need to be taught.

Your first attempt at analyzing difficulties in the area of receptive language centers around pinpointing the behavior. To simply say the child does not respond to instructions is not a sufficient amount of information to plan a treatment program. If you wish the child to respond to verbal cues, then it becomes very important for you to specify which cues. If you are very careful about pinpointing the cues, to which you wish the child to respond, there are some things that will probably become immediately clear to you. First, most of us when dealing with a child provide him with an excess of information concerning what we would like for him to do. For example, we might say to the child, "Jimmy, pick up your toys, put them in the box and come over here and sit down." You have just given four separate cues for four separate behaviors, and if the child does not understand any one of them, he will not be able to do all the things you ask.

A good rule of thumb to use when teaching a child something for the first time is to use a single, exaggerated cue for the one behavior you have pinpointed. A good way to accomplish this is to give the child a verbal cue as slowly and as clearly as possible and at the same time use as many gestures as you can to show the child what the single behavior is that you want him to demonstrate.

CUES

After you have pinpointed the behavior that you wish the child to learn, you should then set up situations to work on those specific tasks. For example, if you wish to teach the verbal cue of "Close the door," then you should set up a practice session working on that concept alone. In all cases you should be very careful that you are using consistent cues. You should not, at least in the beginning, tell the child one time to "close the door" and the next time to "shut the door." Consistency in language is extremely important if the child is going to learn to respond to specific cues. It may be very important at a later stage that the child be able to respond to both "close" and "shut"; however, in the initial stages of training each should be taught separately. In teaching the concept of "close the door," you will want to give the instructions very clearly and possibly place your hand on the child's hand and gently help him push the door closed.

REINFORCEMENT

As is often the case when dealing with receptive language, *the reinforcement for the child is the result of his behavior.* To use the previous example, if you have given the child the instructions, "Close the door," and he successfully completes that task, even with your help the fact that the door is closed is usually a sufficient amount of reinforcement to strengthen that behavior. However, when the result of the behavior is not a sufficient reinforcement then we must resort to some of the other tactics that were described earlier. This will usually consist of saying to the child, "Good, you shut the door," and giving smiles, hugs and attention or other known reinforcements.

SPECIAL TECHNIQUES

One of the tasks that you may be interested in is expanding the child's receptive language ability by responding to more cues in his environment. If this is the case, then you should make yourself a preliminary list of those things to which you wish the child to respond. The list should be kept small at first and consist of those things in his immediate environment. For example, you might like him to be able to identify objects around the house such as a stove, a chair, a light, shoes, a window, etc. You should then set up a practice session dealing with the identification of these objects. Remember to use consistent cues and ask the child to "show you" or to "point to," but in the initial sessions do not mix the two types of instructions. As he becomes proficient in identifying these objects you might then wish to introduce a different cue such as "where" is the stove, or "find" the stove, or "touch" the stove or some other series of instructions you wish him to learn.

You may find that it is easier to expand the range of objects by cutting out a series of pictures of the various objects from a magazine and placing them on the floor in front of the child and asking him to choose one. This is a little more abstract, and real objects should be used in the beginning of training; however, it is a good technique for expanding the child's environment without having him experience the objects.

In review there are a few critical things which you must be aware of when you are dealing with receptive language. First, the initial training program should consist of a single cue and a single behavior for which you use as much exaggeration as possible. It is often helpful in the beginning to have the child imitate something that you do by first saying, "Do this." Second, you should use a consistent set of instructions and be very careful to examine if the reason the child is not responding is because you are giving too many cues of a subtle nature and of different types. Third, be sure that there is some consequence for the child's behaving. Give the child feedback as to the correctness of his performance. In most cases, this feedback or reinforcement will also have to be in an exaggerated form to communicate to the child that what he just did was correct.

EXPRESSIVE LANGUAGE

It is not the intent of this chapter to train you to be a speech therapist; however, there are a variety of things that you can do that will greatly enhance the child's ability to verbally express himself. Frequently children develop a language of their own or at least one that can be only understood by the immediate family. If this is the only way that the child can communicate, at least this is a beginning, but we should not be satisfied with this level of performance.

PINPOINTING THE BEHAVIOR

There are several kinds of deficits that can appear in the form of expressive language problems. First, there can be a general deprivation of words. When this is the case, your task is to increase the number of objects or things that the child can name. The other frequent type of problem is that the child can name a variety of objects but his speech is so unclear that only members of the family can occasionally recognize the word.

CUES

When clarity of words is the problem, then you must try to teach the child how to make the various sounds. This frequently will require that you show the child the correct tongue, teeth, mouth placement to be able to say the word. It will help you pinpoint the behavior by saying the word yourself and examining the relationship of the various parts of your mouth. If the sound that you wish to teach is the sound of the letter "L," then stand in front of the child and exaggerate your mouth movement as much as possible and have the child imitate those mouth movements *without the sound at first*. For example, you open your mouth, put your tongue at the top of your mouth and thrust the tongue downward. Let the child also practice these in front of a mirror so that he can see the relationship of his tongue to yours. In some cases you may have to do this for every letter in the alphabet.

Silence Is Not Always Golden 157

The next step you should take is to put two sounds together. You can do this by putting any two sounds together that you wish after you have taught him the sounds individually. Once the child is able to produce the sound, then you

should require that he use that sound to obtain any item that he wants that has that sound in it. A good example is the child who says "wa-wa" for water and you practice him on the ability to make the "r" sound. When he can successfully do this and imitate your saying "water" then you should demand that he begin saying the word correctly to obtain a drink.

REINFORCEMENT

For many children the reinforcement for this type of activity is simply being able to hear themselves imitate you correctly. However, when this is not the case, you must again resort to some reinforcement system that gives the child feedback as to whether he is right or wrong. Make your cues for the sound that you want him to produce as clear as possible. Exaggerate your mouth movement and exaggerate the way in which you make the sound and give him consistent cues.

When the major problem is not a clarity problem, but just increasing the number of words in the child's vocabulary, this can be done very similarly to the procedure suggested above for working with receptive language. In other words, present the child with a wide variety of objects and ask him to imitate them after you name them. You should again start with those objects most familiar to him around the house and expand to a variety of objects from other environments that can easily be gathered from places like magazines or books. Again, a good strategy for providing the child with reinforcement for using his newly found word is to make that object available to him after he says the word. In many cases this will not be practical and when this is the case you should respond by saying, "You're right. That is a boat."

SPECIAL TECHNIQUES

One strategy that is often employed is to show the child a picture that has many things occurring. Ask the child to describe that picture. You may find at first he can only name various objects in the picture. At that point you should then describe the various things or tell a story and have the child imitate you. You can use these pictures several times to teach the child a variety of descriptive phrases.

Another strategy that can be employed along with this procedure is for you to tell a story about the picture except the most obvious part and let the child tell you that part. Then the next time, tell the child about three-fourths of the story and let him complete it. You can proceed along these lines until you are only telling half the story, then a fourth of the story, and so on until the child is able to describe the activities in detail from the picture along without your help.

There are some very specific rules to remember in both receptive and expressive language.

Break the behavior down into small parts and remember to keep the cues clear and exaggerated.

When the child has demonstrated to you that he can in fact say a particular sound or word, then you should demand that he use that in all appropriate situations and do not let him revert back to a lower stage of communication that was previously successful for him. If you only respond to this newly found level of performance, he will soon understand that this is the way he must now communicate to get the environment to respond to his demands.

Examine the tasks that you are teaching very carefully and be sure to break them down into the smallest steps possible insuring that the child can move from one step to another with maximum success.

KEEPING TRACK

Keeping track can be a very involved process in language training. Some programs have been developed which provide elaborate record-keeping techniques. For most parents, this type of record keeping may be an arduous task. We recommend, therefore, that only a simple record be maintained to ensure that all members of the family require the child to verbalize when he is capable of uttering the appropriate sounds. Initially, words or sounds that he can speak might be recorded in a prominent place in the house. All members of the family should be instructed to insist that the child perform the verbalization before an object is delivered to the child. For instance, if the child can say "cookie," no cookie should be given him until he says the word.

Chapter 13

Walk, Run, Throw and Catch

or

SPECIAL OLYMPICS

"HERE I COME"

THERE ARE TWO areas where handicapped children usually show that they are, in fact, handicapped—language and motor development.

Motor development includes the acquisition of motor skills ranging from the very basic skills of crawling and walking to the more highly complex skills of jumping, throwing and catching a ball. Thus, the parent of a handicapped child may be concerned about his child learning any one of a whole range of skills. Obviously, this short chapter cannot instruct you how to teach all motor skills. Hopefully, it will impart to you some principles which you can apply to any motor skills you desire to teach.

Let us examine three areas of motor development and hope that the examples shown and the techniques described in these three areas will allow you to generalize the principles to any motor area. We shall attempt to show you some techniques for teaching a child to walk, for teaching a child manipulative skills which will help to improve his motor coordination, and we shall show you how to teach a child to throw and catch a ball.

TEACHING THE CHILD TO WALK

Pinpointing and Analyzing the Behavior

There is no problem here for the parent to pinpoint the behavior that they want the child to achieve. They want the child to be able to take steps by himself without holding on to anyone or anything. Each additional step which the child achieves will be an advancement of the behavior and thus the behavior can be analyzed step by step.

Before one can teach the child to walk, the child should have been taught or should be exhibiting standing behavior. Ideally, the child should have been able to pull himself to a standing position holding on to the side of his crib, a table, or a chair, or somebody's hand.

Cues

The person who is to assist the child to walk will use a one inch thick piece of rubber hose which the child will hold. The hose should be approximately 24 inches long and the adult assisting the child should hold the hose initially right next to the child's hand.

Verbal cues of "Walk, Susie," or "Let's see you walk, Johnny," should also be used.

Reinforcement

Ideally, one should have two people assisting a child to walk, one who helps the child through the initial stages and the other who dispenses reinforcement. We strongly urge the use of primary reinforcement—the child's favorite food—when the child is first learning to take a few steps. One person will sit at a specified location in the room and when the child reaches that person, he will give the child primary reinforcement and both adults will provide the child social praise.

However, if only one person is teaching the child to walk, that person should place the primary reinforcement in a position where they can quickly dispense it after the child takes the required number of steps.

Special Techniques

Standing, the child, holding on to the hose with one hand, should be placed about one step away from the person with the reinforcement. The child then is encouraged to take that first step and if necessary the adult should assist him to do so by moving his foot. As soon as the child takes the first step, he receives his reinforcement, both primary and social.

This process is repeated a number of times, always with the child holding on to the hose and with the adult holding on to the hose next to the child's hand. The child is then placed two steps away from the reinforcement with the hands in the same position on the hose. After the child traverses the distance, he receives the reinforcement. The child is then placed three steps, four steps and five steps with each succeeding try, having to go a little further towards the reinforcement.

When the child is able to walk across the room with the adult's hand next to his holding the hose, the adult then slides his hand approximately six inches away from the child's hand and they walk across the room in that manner.

After the child demonstrates that he is capable of traversing the room with the hose held in that manner, the distance from the adult's hand to the child's hand is increased to 12 inches, then 18 inches. Finally, the adult takes the end of the hose and holds it between his two fingers with the child's hand still firmly grasping the hose. Once again, the room is traversed a number of times until the child demonstrates that he has the capability of walking across the room in that manner.

Finally, the adult merely touches the hose with his hand and the child negotiates across the room. At this point in time the child is in essence walking by himself. The adult's hand provides nothing more than a certain amount of assurance to the child.

The next step is for the child to hold the hose by himself and walk across the room. Finally the child is to walk across the room without the hose. The child has learned to walk.

Keeping Track

No involved record keeping is necessary here. It might be well, however, to make a small chart with six columns, one labeled "Hand Next to Child," the next three labeled "Hand 6 Inches From Child," 12 inches and 18 inches, the next column labeled "Adult's Hand at End of Hose," and the final column labeled "Adult Merely Touching the Hose." Then estimate the number of steps that it might take to have the child cross the room in which he is going to practice his walking and down the left-hand side of the paper put the numbers 1, 2, 3, 4, 5, 6 and so on up to the number of steps that you think it will take for the child to traverse the room. As the child succeeds in taking these steps put a checkmark in the appropriate column next to the correct number of steps. This will allow you to see the progress of the child and to allow others in the family to know how well the child is doing and what they can expect. (The following is an illustration of chart.)

	Hand Next To Child	Hand 6" From Child	Hand 12" From Child	Hand 18" From Child	Adult's Hand at End of Hose	Adult Merely Touching the Hose
1.						
2.						
3.						
4.						
5.						
6.						
etc.						

IMPROVING COORDINATION

Seeing the handicapped child walk and watching him cross a room or move up and down steps or run to meet his father when he comes home from work is oftentimes a gratifying experience. If you have had to labor long hours to accomplish this ability in the child, your task is probably not complete yet because as your child grows older you may observe that his coordination is somewhat limited. He may have difficulty manipulating small objects with his fingers or he may walk in a clumsy fashion and you as a parent may say, "Is there anything that I can do about it?"

There has been a number of programs established which have produced very good results in improving the fine motor coordination of a handicapped child. These programs have essentially concentrated on either producing manipulative skills with hands or improving the child's eye-foot coordination, that is his ability to place his foot where he wants to and how he wants to on the ground. A number of simple devices and techniques are available for the parents who want to assist the child in improving these motor areas.

EYE-HAND COORDINATION

Pinpointing Behavior and Analyzing Behavior

When saying that we wish to improve eye-hand coordination in a child, we are talking about very broad and very general types of behavior for there are all types of manipulative skills which the child will need to develop with his hands. It is often best to actually teach the child the particular manipulative skills which we may want to achieve, such as threading a needle, sorting objects and so on. But there is some evidence also to indicate that the ability to do one small motor task with one's hands generalizes to a number of other small motor tasks. For instance, the child who is able to put small pegs in tiny holes is also able to place other objects in other small areas and the child who is able to walk a straight line placing one foot behind the other usually has little difficulty in placing his feet in the exact position on the ground where he may want them. Thus, in this particular section we shall talk about two methods of actually improving eye-hand coordination with toys with the realization that if the child is able to accomplish the ultimate tasks described herein he will in fact then be able to do other manipulative types of tasks.

Cues and Special Techniques

Let us first examine some techniques for improving eye-hand coordination or manipulative skills. A number of devices are available commercially and are marketed as educational toys which can be helpful in this area. Perhaps if Dad is a handy man, he might be able to construct some of these toys for the child.

We are sure that you are all familiar with the rings and pegs which are available commercially. If you are going to present these to the child to improve his eye-hand coordination, start with a peg that is stationary, not one that rocks. Present to the child only one ring, and let him achieve success with that one ring. If it is obvious to you that this is a very difficult task for the child, remove the ring and substitute a mason lid jar top or a bracelet or any other round object that has a wider hole than the one of the ring that you bought.

Once the child masters that skill with the wider ring, then go to the narrower hole ring and then let him try to put that on. Once he succeeds in doing that, then present him the remainder of the rings for placement on the pegs. The next step might be a peg which rocks back and forth, a rather popular commercial toy.

Another excellent eye-hand coordination exercise are pegs being placed in holes. There are various size peg and hole sets available commercially although this is a very easy thing for Dad to make with a drill and the purchase of various size dowels at the hardware store. Dad can make a number of small peg boards with different size holes in each one. You see illustrated three different types of boards each containing a number of different size pegs. The thinner the peg to be placed in the wider holes, of course, the easier the task. Start with a large size hole and a small size peg and have your child place these in the peg board. Also, start with just one hole and just one peg. Cover the remainder with masking tape. You see illustrated a board ready for the child to start. Notice that the board has a large hole and that the child is going to place in it a relatively thin peg. When the child demonstrates that he is able to place this thin peg in the large hole, remove the masking tape from the other holes and provide him the remainder of the pegs and let him perfect his ability.

Once you are satisfied that he has mastered this task, provide him with a slightly thicker sized peg.

When he has completed this task, then he is ready to move on to smaller holes and smaller pegs until he is actually manipulating pegs that are nothing more than the size of toothpicks and placing them in very fine holes.

Reinforcement

Both of the above are examples of ways in which to assist your child in improving his eye-hand motor coordination. Notice that in each case the task was made as easy as possible for the child and gradually the task was made more difficult and more extensive. This is an essential principle in teaching motor behavior to any child. Never expect too much too fast. Many a little league ball player has failed to make it to the diamond because Dad pushed just a little bit too hard.

Reinforcement with these tasks, of course, should follow the same principles as for other tasks which you have tried. Initially, reinforce the child with each ring or each peg that he places in the hole. As he develops proficiency with the pegs and with the rings require him to place two, three or four before you reinforce him. Both the peg toys and the rings allow for this gradual extension of tasks before reinforcement. In the case of the rings, the child was putting on one ring and then was reinforced, then he was required to put on two, then three and then four. In the case of the pegs, only one hole is left open for the child, he puts the peg in and is reinforced. When two holes were exposed, he had to place two of them in before being reinforced, and then three, and four and so on.

Keeping Track

There is no need here to keep any pencil and paper track of the child's performance in these tasks. This can be easily accounted for by just knowing how many rings that you leave on the post. This number will indicate how many rings the child is able to do. By examining the pegboard, noticing the number of peg holes that have been exposed tells you how many pegs the child is able to place on the pegboard.

Eye-Foot Coordination

Improving the coordination of a child's hands and his ability to manipulate objects is a somewhat easier task than improving his coordination with his feet. It is easier for your hands to manipulate a child's hands to assist him in initial stages; it is more difficult for you to manipulate the child's feet because of the balance problem. Oftentimes when we try to move a handicapped child's foot, he tends to lose his balance. Therefore, never feel reluctant to have the child hold on to you while he experiments with putting his feet in new directions for the first few times. One such foot exercise is here described.

You recall when you were a child, especially if you grew up in the city, trying to walk or balance yourself on the curb of the sidewalks. If you grew up in the country, perhaps you can recall trying to balance yourself as you walked on top of a fence. Children have a natural desire to balance and move their feet in a very precise way over narrow objects and demonstrate that they have good balance. A handicapped child will enjoy this type of activity also. However, with handicapped children, this is often a much more difficult task, and so, like

Walk, Run, Throw and Catch 173

the hand manipulative exercises that we recommended, the foot exercises also are approached so as to provide the child as easy, small task to begin and then gradually lengthening the task and making it more difficult.

Pinpointing and Analyzing Behavior and Cues

Let us suppose that we are trying to get the child to walk heel-to-toe down a six foot length of 1 inch wide tape which we place on the floor. The child tries it and is unable to accomplish the task. Two things should be done. First, the width of the line should be markedly widened so that the child's foot easily fits within the line. It is not unusual to widen it to as much as nine inches. Secondly, the length of the line is reduced so that the child only need take one step to reach the end of the line.

Reinforcement

Once the child takes that one step, we reinforce him and tell him how well he is doing. When he can do this well, we extend the length of the line so that he has to take two steps and then three steps and gradually as many as ten steps before reinforcement.

Special Techniques

When he is able to walk the thick line ten steps without stepping off of it, we begin to narrow the line. For instance,

if we started with a nine inch wide line, we would reduce it to seven inches then five inches then to three inches and finally to one inch lines. With each reduction in width we would see if the child were able to walk the length of the narrower line.

If he were not, we would then once again reduce the length of the line so that he would only have to take one step on it, then two, then three and so on.

Keeping Track

Keeping track of walking on various widths, of course, again requires no pencil or paper. The size of the tape that we have placed on the floor tells us what width tape we are using. Marks placed on the tape with a black grease pencil will then tell us how far the child is able to walk or where we should begin with him.

The above exercises for improving eye-hand coordination and eye-foot coordination are only a sample of the type of things that you can do with your child. This book is not meant to be a treatise on the total range of improving motor coordination but it does hope to present to the parent some techniques which hopefully they will be able to use and apply to other motor tasks which they may be trying to teach their child.

PLAYING BALL

It is true that some handicapped children will probably never learn to play ball well enough to play in little league baseball or football. However, many of them can learn to play that well and many of them can participate in team sports. The place to begin teaching a handicapped child how to handle a ball is to teach him to throw and to catch.

THROWING BALL

Pinpointing and Analyzing Behavior

Behavior which we want the child, of course, to achieve here is to be able to throw the ball accurately to another person at specified distances. In every case we want the child to learn to throw overhand right from the beginning, and so our behavior is an overhand throw.

Cues and Special Techniques

He should be learning to throw with a tennis ball which is an easy ball for the child to grasp and to throw. It may be necessary to take your hand and guide his and show him the motions. The first step once he has learned that motion and learned to let go of the ball at the proper time (and of course being reinforced when he does let go of the ball at the proper time), is to get the child to throw it on a fly at a distance. One might try placing him in the center of a six foot circle and asking him to throw the ball so that it lands beyond the tape or the chalk that you have placed upon the floor to mark the distance of six feet on the fly. The next step is to make his throwing more directional. Carve out a six foot arc on the circle and have him throw so that the ball lands between those two points, then gradually narrow the arc and stand at the far side of it so that the ball is coming to you.

Once he has mastered throwing the ball in a specific direction and with fair accuracy so that you are able to catch it, begin extending the distance beyond six feet, first to seven feet, then to eight feet, then to 10 feet, 12 feet and so on.

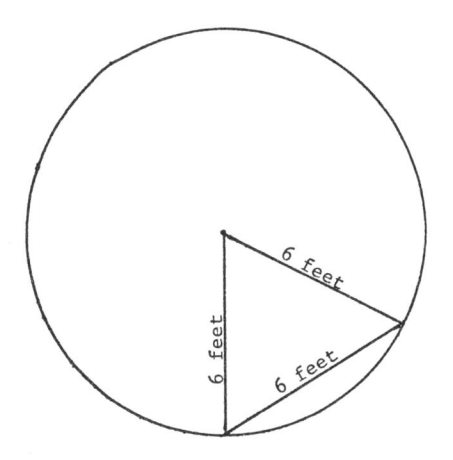

Reinforcement

A child throwing a ball will normally receive such enjoyment from throwing a ball that any reinforcement other than social praise and encouragement from the adult working with the child is usually unnecessary. Primary reinforcement would be extremely difficult to administer, although a system of keeping track of how far the child can throw with accuracy by chalking marks on the sidewalks or driveway where the child is learning to throw might be an excellent reinforcement for some children.

Keeping Track

The chalk marks on the driveway or sidewalks are also an excellent way for the adults to keep track of how far the child is able to throw the ball. If chalk marks are unfeasible, a pencil notation some place indicating how many feet the child is able to throw accurately should be kept so that other members of the family teaching the child how to throw will know how far away to stand from the child.

CATCHING A BALL

Pinpointing and Analyzing Behavior

When one imagines one catching a ball, a number of different configurations of the human body can be envisioned. We can envision an outfielder making a leaping one-handed catch in center field, our favorite short stop catching a hard grounder, or our favorite first baseman stretching to make the catch before the runner gets to base. And so there are one-handed catchers in a number of different positions and there are also a number of two-handed catchers. We shall attempt to teach the child to catch two-handed with the ball generally reaching him somewhere in-between his stomach and shoulders.

Cues

When a child is first being taught to catch, any type of hardball should not be used at all. This includes tennis balls or any other type of rubber ball. A cloth ball about four or five inches in diameter is the ideal size for the child to learn to catch. The reason for the cloth ball as opposed to the rubber ball is that there is a tendency for the rubber ball to bounce off the child's hands and into the child's face, thus causing him to develop a flinching motion when the ball is thrown to him. This flinching motion, of course, will interfere with his catching ability. Even if he were to be hit in the face with the soft cloth ball, it would not hurt him and a flinching reaction would probably not develop.

Special Techniques

Start by having the child catch the cloth ball at a distance of about two feet. Have him place his hands in front of him in a "catch" position. After he has demonstrated that he is able to catch the cloth ball in that position, move back a foot at a time being very careful that the child is able to master four out of five catches before proceeding to the next foot distance.

After you reach the six foot mark, and the child has demonstrated that he can catch the ball 80 percent of the time, substitute a rubber five inch ball and move once again to a close distance of three feet. Have him catch the ball at three feet again striving for an 80 percent success ratio and then once again move back a foot at a time until you reach six feet.

After he has demonstrated that he can catch the five inch ball 80 percent of the time at a distance of six feet, substitute a tennis ball or a like size rubber ball for the five inch ball and once again move to within a distance of three feet from the child. Repeat the whole process until you reach the six foot level and then gradually begin extending the distance with the child.

Reinforcement

Once again, you are reminded that every time the child catches the ball initially you want to reinforce him strongly with verbal praise and be very enthusiastic about his performance. As he gains proficiency the reinforcement need not occur after each catch, but should be provided intermittently so that the child understands that he is doing very well. With throwing and catching a ball, the child himself will begin to understand when he is doing well and this will provide a form of reinforcement which is quite adult—self-reinforcement, the type of reinforcement that we eventually want the child to develop.

Keeping Track

Once again, there is little need to keep any pencil records of how well the child is catching. Marks on the ground are very effective to indicate where the adults and where the child should stand so that one knows the distance at which the child is catching. The type of ball the child is using, left around so that the child can manipulate it in his free time, will indicate to the adult which size ball to use.

And so, whether your child is learning to toddle, or whether he is in need of improvement in his motor coordination, or whether he is on his way to learning how to play ball, remember that in teaching him you must break the behavior down into its smallest parts and teach one part at a time. You must make the task easy enough so that he will achieve success, and when he achieves that success, you must reinforce him with those reinforcers that are most powerful for him, whether they be primary reinforcement or social praise. If you follow these simple rules for whatever motor behavior you are going to teach your child, you will be surprised at how quickly he learns.

Chapter 14

LOOK MOM, I CAN COUNT

or

How to Teach Academics

During the past couple of years we have had the very good fortune of being associated with a preschool teacher who has demonstrated very adequately most of the procedures and techniques described in this book. An area of concern which we have had for a long time was whether children who are moderately and severely retarded can learn any academic skills, such as recognition of letters and words; and whether they can develop an ability to use numbers, that is count, add and subtract. We are now convinced, based on our experience with this preschool class and other similar classes, that the majority of moderately and severely retarded children can learn many more academic skills than we have previously given them credit for.

We believe strongly that the more skills which you can give an individual and the more learning that you can impart to him, the greater the chances for that individual to find happiness and adjust to his circumstances. This holds true for handicapped people as well as normal people. We believe that the handicapped person who can read or who can use numbers has skills which may allow him to hold jobs. This in turn may give him more happiness than a position in a sheltered workshop or no job at all. Thus, we have not been reluctant to teach academic skills to moderately and severely retarded children. Moreover, we have found that we have achieved a large measure of success with very young children. Our studies have not been going on long enough to determine the long-range effects of this academic training, but the initial results are very promising.

For instance, in the preschool class that we have just mentioned, a sight reading program was underway at the time of this writing which started in November and lasted through February. As a result of this program, one four-year-old mongoloid boy could recognize 28 different words. Two other children, both age five and both classified as brain damaged, can recognize more than 15 words. Another four-year-old mongoloid had developed in the same period a reading vocabulary of 10 words. This was all achieved in the preschool setting with effort not exceeding ten minutes a day. Many of these preschool children can recognize the names of their classmates; a number of them less than six years old have begun to learn letters of the alphabet. Most have learned to rote count and at least in two instances children are able to count up to ten.

One must realize that there is nothing special about this class, except that the teacher uses very faithfully the principles espoused in this book. The teacher also has not prejudged the capabilities of the children and limited what they can learn by refusing to teach them certain things; the teacher has maintained an open mind and operated on the principle that she really did not know how much the children could learn, but was willing to try to teach the children anything a normal child of their age could learn. Results are indicating some very startling developments and demonstrate to us that the retarded child is probably capable of a much higher level of reading performance than we are teaching in the majority of our schools. Other studies with older children indicate that they too have many academic capabilities. For instance, in one study conducted by one of the authors of this book (Brodsky) reading skills were successfully imparted to adults up to 32 years old.

In this chapter we follow the same format which we have utilized in the previous chapters about specific skills. We are focusing on two behaviors—the writing of a letter and rote counting to number 10. These, of course, are only representative of many academic skills.

PINPOINTING THE BEHAVIOR

Pinpointing behavior for an academic task is sometimes the most difficult not only for parents but also for teachers. For instance, one often hears a teacher saying that she is going to teach a child the letters of the alphabet. When asked what she means by that, the teacher says, "Well, I'm going to teach him to read the letters" or "I'm going to teach him to write the letters" or "I'm going to teach him the sound of the letters." When one considers that there are 26 letters in each of those three skills, reading writing and sounding, one sees at least three times 26 or 78 different learning tasks. This does not take into consideration that there are more than one sound for each letter, or that there are probably three or four different ways to write or read a letter. For instance, as an adult in our society you cope with a block capital "A," a script capital a (*A*), a small script letter a (*a*), and two types of printed small letter "a"'s (a and *a*). Thus for just the letter "a" there are five variations which you might have to learn how to read or to write. If you go back to our chapter on pinpointing and analyzing behavior, you will recall that each of these is probably one complex learning task, and, of course, if we are going to teach a child to break down each of those writing behaviors we may have a number of subtasks.

For purposes of discussion in this chapter, we are going to imagine that you are teaching the child to write the letter "A." Not only have you designated that he is to write the letter "A," but that you are going to designate a block capital letter "A." Thus the complex behavior has been pinpointed.

As we look at this complex behavior, however, we see that writing of the block letter "A" requires at least a number of distinct tasks. First, of course, we should have determined that the child can hold a pencil. Second, we should have determined that the child knows how to make marks on a paper with a pencil. Having insured ourselves that the child has these two skills, we are then ready to teach him to write the letter "A." We break the letter "A" into at least three parts. If the child is having special difficulty in mastering these parts,

184   *Isn't It Time He Outgrew This?*

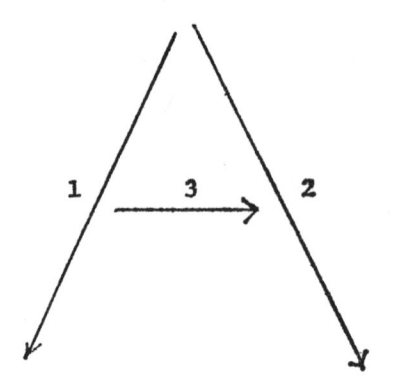

Three Parts

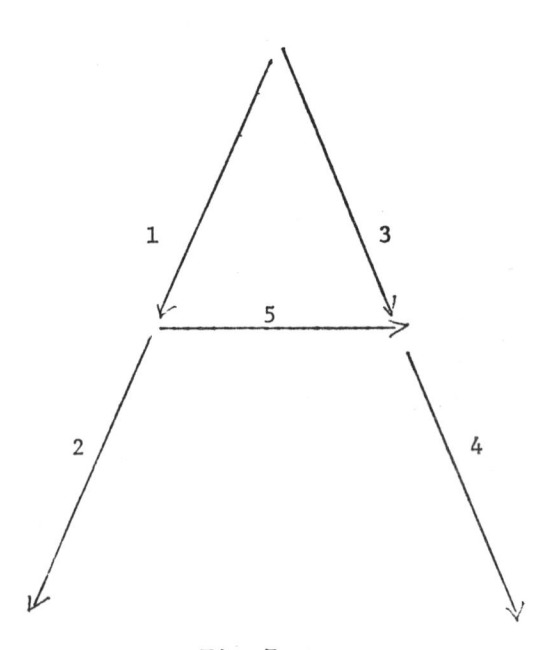

Five Parts

(Arrows show direction of pencil movement.)

Parts of the letter "A."

we might analyze the behavior by breaking it down into five distinct steps as follows. Thus, each of these three or five steps becomes a separate learning task. We have now pinpointed the behavior, analyzed it and pinpointed the simple behaviors or little behaviors that make up the complex behavior.

For purposes of this chapter, let us look at another academic task. Most parents, initially, are concerned with their children being "able to count." Once again, there are a number of tasks involved in this phrase. By able to count do you mean that you want the child to be able to recite one through 10? through 20? or higher? Does being able to count mean being able to count various objects? If so, how high do you want the child to be able to count these objects?—3? 5? 10? 100? 1,000? In other words what specific behavior do you want him to be able to do when you say you want him to be able to count?

The place to begin is probably teaching the child to rote count—that is, being able to just recite numbers one after the other. Knowing the sequnce of numbers is usually a prerequisite for being able to count objects. This does not mean, however, that the child cannot be pointing to objects as he recites the numbers. Let us pinpoint the behavior to be learned by saying we want the child to be able to rote count to ten. Now even here we have a very complex behavior, for there are essentially ten learning steps which are chained together. But at least we have designated a terminal behavior desired, and we are willing to look now at all the little subbehaviors that make up this complex behavior. For instance, the child will have to learn how to count "one, two" before he learns how to count "one, two, three." Knowing that these are separate learning steps, we are probably ready to teach.

CUES

How does one get a child to write the letter "A"? First, one should realize that I have chosen the letter "A" because a particular boy I am going to teach is named Alphonse, and "A" happens to be the first letter in Alphonse's name. If the child were named Timmy, I should teach him to write the letter "T" first. And if her name were Susy, I should teach her to write the letter "S" first. Thus, I think that the child's name itself provides a very powerful and "child-like" cue for the child who is learning to write letters. In other words, teach the child the letters of his name first.

In the case of Alphonse, I can say to Alphonse, "Let us write "A" for Alphonse," and knowing that Alphonse may have some difficulty learning to write the letter, I have divided the steps into five learning stages. The first is where Alphonse just completes the cross bar in the letter "A" following the dotted lines, and so I present to him a letter "A" written in this manner. The careful reader of this book should realize that what we are doing is reverse chaining the teaching of the writing of the letter "A." There are a number of different places where this can be written: on a blackboard; on a sheet of paper covered by acetate so the child can use grease pencil and erase with kleenex and thus repeat the task a number of times; paper; and certainly the letter can be presented to him in a variety of sizes. To make the task interesting I might present it to him in a number of different ways. I would certainly, though, accompany the presentation with a verbal cue, "Let's write 'A' for Alphonse." Initially, he would be presented the letter with dotted lines to follow. These would eventually be faded out as the child developed skill writing the letter, but this fading process would not begin until he had been able to follow the dotted lines through all of the five steps needed to complete "A."

When teaching the child rote counting, I must make a choice. I can teach him by presenting to him one, two, three, four, five, six, seven, eight, nine, and he just says 10. Or I can start by having him repeat one and then one, two, and then one, two, three. These authors have found much more success by letting the child say the last words in a series. For instance, using this method a child can be taught rhymes, his prayers and numerous other recitations. For cues I probably would say

Look Mom, I Can Count

The Five Steps

Initial presentation of letter "A."

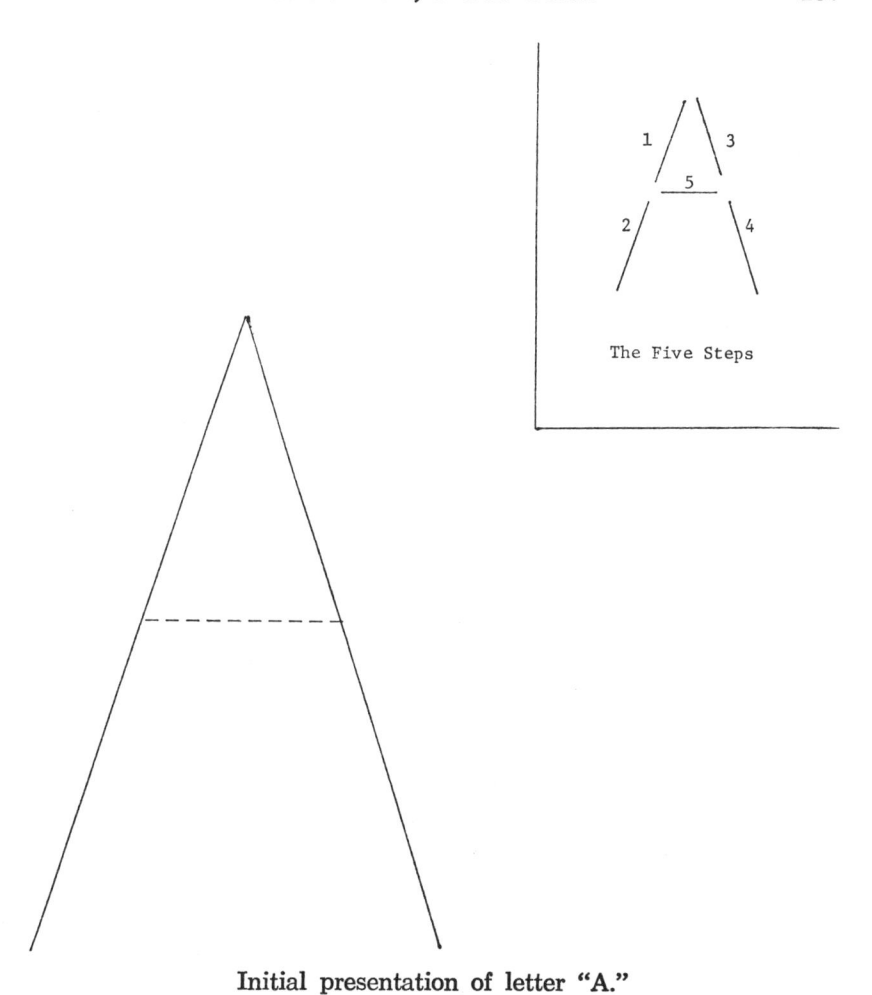

"let us count," and might have the child counting on his fingers, and we might count together 1-2-3-4-5-6-7-8-9 and I would stop and I would get him to say 10. I would repeat this a number of times until he was able to say 10 by himself.

Fingers are very handy cues, although blocks, toy cars, objects around the room and a number of other things can be used to assist the child in counting.

REINFORCEMENT

With both of these tasks, reverse chaining is recommended. For instance, with the letter "A," the task would initially be presented to the child in this manner. When the child completed the last step of the letter "A," he would be reinforced. Social reinforcement ("I like the way you write the letter "A"; or a big hug or kiss), primary reinforcement (cereal bits, M&Ms) or other tangible reinforcements are all appropriate. Remember that social reinforcement must be administered with any tangible reinforcer, and that reinforcement is to be administered only at the end of the chain.

Also remember that when the child is starting a new task, it is well to give the child reinforcement each time that he performs the task. When the child begins to master the task, it probably will not be necessary to give him reinforcement each time he accomplishes the task, but reinforcement may be administered every third or fourth time.

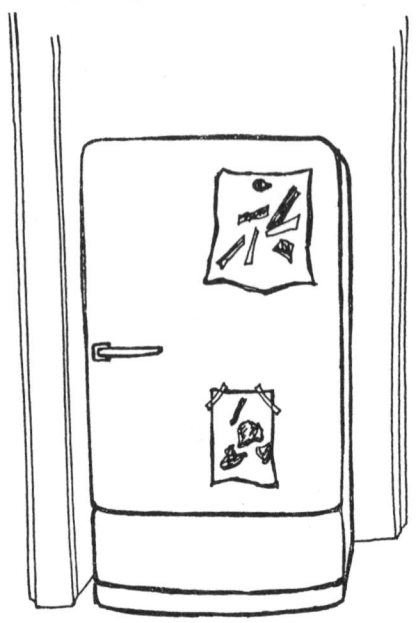

In the case of the child who is learning to write or learning to cut, or learning to paste, a very effective reinforcement which parents can use and which pleases most young children is the posting of the child's work in a prominent place in the home. It is interesting to visit some of the homes of preschool children with whom we have been associated and with whom these methods have been used. In almost every home, the child's work at school and at home is very visibly displayed. In one home the child's success with cutting out strips of paper were displayed by taking the colored strips of paper and pasting them to a white sheet of paper in a random fashion and posting them on the refrigerator door. The asthetic value in the kitchen may not have been to an interior decorator's liking, but the effect upon the child was obvious. His mother would post his work on the refrigerator door during the day; when his father returned home from work, the child would lead him by the hand and point to his accomplishments of the day, thus receiving further reinforcement in the form of praise from the father.

SPECIAL TECHNIQUES

Before teaching a child to learn how to write, we have already determined that the child has some skills which include being able to hold the pencil and being able to make marks on a piece of paper. Even with these skills it may be necessary to look at the size of the pencil being used. Young children oftentimes work better holding a fat pencil. This is known as a primary pencil and is available in most stores.

Other than pencil and paper, many children are fascinated with the idea of writing on the blackboard. This should be encouraged. Perhaps a model of the letter on which the child is working should be drawn on the top of the blackboard where the child cannot erase it; thus he will have the opportunity to copy it during his play activities. Whenever you see him doing this, of course, be sure to stop what you are doing and reinforce him and praise him for his writing on the blackboard.

We have found that making paper and pencil readily available to the child will assist him in learning to write faster. We suggest setting up a small child's table with a container that might hold a pencil or crayon and leaving paper by it. You will find that the child frequently will sit at the table, take out his pencil and write on the paper. Again when you see him doing this be sure to reinforce him and praise him for his writing efforts.

Many parents are reluctant to leave pencils in easy reach of children. They feel that the child will write on the walls or write on the table. And the child may well do this. However, the chances are slight of him doing it when both pencil and paper are available to him and he is being reinforced for writing on the paper. The reinforcement will keep him writing on the paper instead of the wall. Moreover, writing on the wall or writing on the table or other inappropriate places is a behavior that can be cured or extinguished just as are other inappropriate behaviors (refer to the chapter on behavior problems).

When teaching a child to count, we have already mentioned that you should take every opportunity to have the child practice his counting. For instance, if you have steps in your home as the child is going up or down, count each step. Count the blocks as the child puts them away. Count the number of cookies mother is making. Count the number of potatoes she cooked. Count the number of chairs around the table. Have the child count out spoons to be placed around the table at dinner time. There are countless instances where a child in the daily course of activities around the home can practice his counting without mother stopping all that she is doing to help him do this. Having the child count in this manner, you will also be improving his language ability. He will be responding to such questions as "How many cookies are there?," "How many chairs around the table?"

Oftentimes when parents become engaged in teaching their child academic skills and the child chooses not to participate on that day, the parent gets very "uptight" and concerned. Instead the action for the parent should be to find reinforcers which will be more powerful for the child and will cause him to want to participate in the academic tasks. Children, just as all human beings, oftentimes get tired of receiving the same reinforcement. It is necessary to change it periodically, and if you find your child becoming bored or not interested or listless or refusing to do tasks that you have designated for him, he is ready for a new reinforcement. Your task as the teacher and the parent is to find another reinforcement which will cause him to want to do the task or perform the behavior again.

KEEPING TRACK

Keeping track of a child's ability to perform writing skills in letters of the alphabet is relatively easy. Once having determined what the steps are in writing each letter, one lists those steps or illustrates them on a sheet of paper as we have done in the illustration. We have included in this illustration the process of fading out the dots and thus the whole process takes nine steps.

As the child demonstrates a mastery of each step of the process, the parent can place a check mark in the appropriate box indicating that the child has learned the skills and is ready to move on to the next skill. You will notice that we have listed the skill in a reverse chain order, thereby indicating that the child has learned step nine, eight, and seven, and is now on step six.

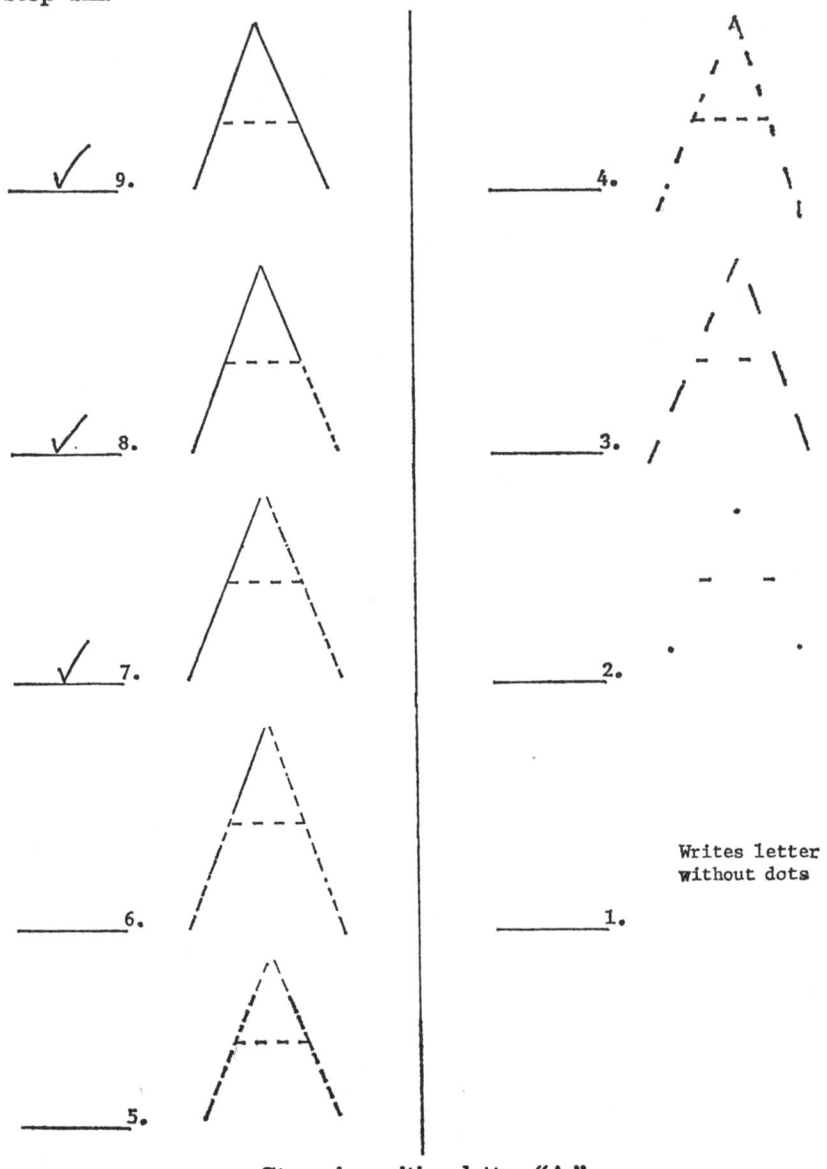

Steps in writing letter "A."

Writes letter without dots

In the case of counting, if the child is learning to count in a forward chain manner, 1-2-3-etc., a good device for keeping track as well as reinforcing the child is to cut out large numbers and tape them in some prominent space as the child acquires the learning of the number. This can also be done on a reverse chain procedure where the number 10 is first posted, then the number 9, then the number 8, and so on.

If, however, you do not desire to post the numbers, a memorandum or note is usually necessary to yourself placed in a frequently sighted place to remind you at what level the child should be counting all by himself.

CASE HISTORY I

You are the parent of Tommy Jones and you feel that Tommy is ready to learn to recognize the letters of his alphabet. What is the first thing that you must do to teach Tommy the recognition of these letters, and how do you break down the learning tasks?

Case History I—Answer

The first thing that must be done is that I must determine what letters I am going to teach Tommy first. I decide that I will teach him the letters of his name so that he will be able to recognize them and perhaps eventually spell his name. Therefore, the first letter that I am going to teach Tommy is the letter "T."

I must also decide what type of letter "T" I am going to teach Tommy. I decide that I will teach him small "t" as it appears in a printed book so that, hopefully, he will eventually be able to recognize the name Tommy in and on a printed page or recognize the letters t-o-m-m-y on a printed page. Since small letters appear more often than capital letters, I have chosen the small letters. The next thing I must decide is how I will present the letters to Tommy. I have chosen the flash card method, where I have written the letter "t" on a card, hold it up to Tommy and say "Tommy what is this?" and I want him to reply, "The letter 't'."

I must also decide what types of reinforcement I am going to use. Tommy loves chocolate wafers so I am going to give him a piece of chocolate wafer each time he correctly identifies the letter "t." I am going to combine this with social praise, saying something like "I like the way you can say the letter 't'." I have further decided relative to reinforcement that if he recognizes the letter "t" three times in succession, I shall move to the next letter, "o," and reinforce recognition of the letter "t" with primary reinforcement only about every fourth or fifth time although I shall reinforce with primary reinforcement every time he recognizes the letter "o." When I move to the letter "m," I will reinforce the letter "t" only with social reinforcement, the letter "o" with primary reinforcement every fourth or fifth time and the letter "m" every time. And so, I have also scheduled the way I shall fade out reinforcement.

I shall keep track of Tommy's progress by posting a brightly colored letter "t" on the refrigerator door after he learns to recognize it. I shall do the same for each subsequent letter, thereby spelling out his name.

CASE HISTORY II

My name is Martha Mother and my son, James, is learning to write his numbers. He knows how to write one, two and three. We are now learning to write number four and suddenly he no longer wants to write. What should I do to get him to continue to write? Every time I suggest to him that we should do our homework and do our writing he says "no" and begins to pout.

Case History II—Answer

Martha Mother should look at the reinforcements that she is using for her son, James. Obviously the reinforcements are no longer strong enough for him. She may have been using the same reinforcement too long and James became tired of it, or satiated. Therefore, it is time to find a more powerful reinforcement.

Chapter 15

"AW MOM, DO I HAVE TO ???"

or

How to Set Up a Token System

MOST OF THIS BOOK has been written for the younger child or for the more severely handicapped child. This chapter is concerned with the older and less-handicapped child. We shall present some methods for coping with the frequent everyday behavorial problems of the adolescent and pre-adolescent child. The child we will describe in this chapter has problems with self-help skills; but the problems are of a different type than the younger child. This child has probably mastered nearly all the self-help skills. He can make his bed perfectly well as long as you are there. But left to himself his bed usually goes unmade or is sloppily made. This is not because he doesn't know how, but like all children his age he isn't concerned— or he "forgot."

His behavior problems are not violent temper tantrums. His most upsetting problem is the "Aw Mom, do I have to???"— followed by much sulking, foot-dragging and door-banging.

We also find that parents wish to teach a child of this age certain things, but often are unable to do so. You wish to give him daily and weekly chores to help him develop a sense of responsibility. Perhaps you bought him a dog because he promised to feed him daily and *always* take care of him. But if feeding were left entirely to him, that dog would have starved long ago.

You also wish him to understand that there are rules that need following: school lessons must be done; he must get home on time from school. But you find the familiar pattern—his failure to perform as you expect and your scolding or punishing him (and then feeling guilty about it) only to have the same thing happen all over again.

What we propose as a remedy to all this is called a "token system." It is essentially a method for motivating children. Despite its apparent simplicity, it has been found to be effective with a wide variety of children—retarded, deaf, blind, physically-handicapped, "normal" and effective in a wide variety of situations—homes, classrooms, institutions, etc.

Tokens are tangible, visible symbols of reinforcement. They resemble coins or paper money in that they are a medium of exchange: they are awarded by you for desired behavior and exchanged back to you for reinforcements. Like money they can be traded for a variety of things. Although they can be awarded immediately during and after the desired behavior, they can be saved for later exchanges. They allow a child to have in his hand tangible proof that he has earned all or part of a reinforcement that he desires. Most of all they allow you to specify clear relationships between behaviors—that is they allow you to specify cues, behaviors and reinforcements—those things necessary for learning to occur.

For a token system to work you must clearly specify to the child the behavior expected, the cues to guide his behavior and the reinforcements to follow the behavior. As a beneficial side-effect, tokens give a child the first-hand experience of choosing among alternatives and saving for future rewards.

The following sections explain in more detail how the token system works and how you can set one up for your child.

Pinpointing and Analyzing Behavior

As you read our definition of a token system you may have thought to yourself that it is really nothing more than a glorified allowance like that which you received when you were a child. The only difference might seem to be that tokens are used instead of money; and your child pays you instead of the local candy store owner or movie theater operator. In most respects you would be right. The major difference is that with a token system you pinpoint the desired behavior and clearly specify the reinforcement. It is really not adequate to say "You'll get your allowance if you are good all week. " Nor is it really good for the child if he earns his allowance only by cutting the grass when there are more important things that he should be learning.

1. In setting up a token system, the first step is to specify behavioral areas of concern. Get a sheet of paper and begin making a list. You may first wish to list things that he ought to do, but does not—like make his bed, do his homework, pick up his clothes.

2. You should identify what we call terminal behaviors or the finished product. What is it we expect our children to do—finally. And how often? Make his bed well—*every day.* Feed the dog—*daily.* Do his homework—*five nights a week.* These are the behaviors you are going to try to develop.

3. Next you will want to specify areas of good behavior that could also be improved. It is usually the case that these behaviors go unreinforced. Some of these things will be the opposite of the things you listed above—making his bed, etc. But there should be many other things; for all of us seem to pay little attention to everyday things when they are good. We just seem to expect a bed to be made and only notice and react when it is not. How often do we praise our children for spending a quiet, well-behaved evening?

4. Now write what your child does *now* in these areas both in terms of quality and frequency. "Make a rumpled bed—twice a week." "Feeds the dog four to five times a week."

Then as clearly as you can write out a good description of the "terminal behaviors." What are the little behaviors and the big BEHAVIORS involved? What makes a well-made bed? Blankets tucked in—top cover turned back—no wrinkles, etc. You can save a lot of later disagreements and confusion by being able to clearly specify to your child what is expected of him. You can avoid such conversations as:

Mother: "Why didn't you make your bed?"
Billy: "I did."
Mother: "No, you didn't."
Billy: "Yes, I did!"
Mother: "That's *not* what *I* call making a bed." etc. etc.

Also by clearly specifying the finished product you are able to rate his daily performance and determine whether he is doing a better job as time goes by.

5. Now look at your list. Compare where your child is now and where you want him to be. The trick is to start requiring behavioral improvement at just above the present level of performance. *Don't demand final performance or the "terminal behavior" immediately!* If he cannot make a bed at all, the first step might be putting on the sheets and covers in the right order.

6. Now arrange the behaviors which you want him to perform in order of the most important to you to the least important or in the order of that which is in most need for improvement to that in least need for improvement.

7. Assign a daily quota of tokens to be earned in each area, with the most to be earned in the areas you have ranked first.

For example, your child may earn five tokens in the behavioral areas that need the most improvement. He might earn two tokens in an area where he usually does well. Be sure to allow enough tokens to be earned in these areas so that you can award less as each area improves. A good attempt at bedmaking could be worth three points out of a possible five. In a week or two this same performance may only be worth one point.

Once you have completed this list you are ready to look at the next essential of the learning process—cues.

CUES

As you look at the terminal behaviors you desire, think about the cues that should prompt these behaviors. You will probably discover that for the most part the behaviors you want to develop will eventually be "self-starting." That is, you want the child to dress himself and make his bed everyday without direction. What will "tell" him to start these behaviors will be a combination of things—the sight of his unmade bed, a new shirt that he wants to wear, etc. If there is a single cue common to all these things it will most likely be "time": He knows school time is 8:30, and his bed must be made before he leaves for school. Nearly all behaviors of this type have to be completed by a certain time. The best approach is to write the time next to each behavior you have listed.

At this point, you may want to make a chart that you can post in a conspicuous place. The chart will now have a list of each behavior you expect, how often it is expected to be done, the time it should be done, and the range of points or tokens to be earned for each behavior. You should give your child a copy of the descriptions of the behaviors and explain it to him.

The chart itself serves as a cue for the child. You may also want to have a place beside each behavior where your child can "sign in" to indicate that the behavior is completed. Eventually this chart, like other cues, can be gradually removed. After a while the child may not have to sign in, but just use the chart as a reminder. You should find that as you progress and fade out these cues, that your child will do things without being reminded and without the gimmicks such as the chart. This indicates that he is making a transition to ADULT CUES, such as telling himself when a job needs doing.

With a more retarded child, the cues may have to be less elaborate. However, we have found that even severely retarded children can learn the token system and respond to it.

REINFORCEMENT

Token systems work because of two reinforcing actions: First they attach reinforcements to behaviors that previously were not reinforced. This insures that your child *will* be reinforced for spending that nice, quiet evening. Also they reverse our all-too-human tendency to react only to the bad behavior. They help us adults to stop complaining when the bed is not made and to stop ignoring the bed that is made. A good job of bed-making now gets rewarded: and bad jobs simply means a lost opportunity to earn reinforcement.

Second: The very act of handing over a token to your child practically guarantees that you are going to interact with him following good behavior. So tokens also teach you to use your attention and enthusiasm more effectively.

The first step is to remember that you are in effect making a contract with your child. You are specifying the behaviors you will reinforce, but he has the last word as to the reinforcements. If you pick things as reinforcement that just are not reinforcing to him, you cannot expect him to perform as you would like. The best approach is for you and your child to pick a number of different things as reinforcements—privileges, TV time, trips, candy, etc. Ask your child what he would like to work for. He may have a number of things in mind that he would love to have. More often than not, these things are quite inexpensive.

Still, many reinforcements will be too expensive to be traded for tokens—like a television set. The best approach here is to rent the use of these things for a certain period of time—ten tokens may buy an hour of TV time, etc.

You can also choose reinforcements for your child by watching what he spends a lot of time doing. Anything that your child spends a lot of time doing (provided he has had a free choice) can be used as a reinforcement—watching TV, playing with friends, etc.

Next set the prices on the reinforcements. You should establish a wide range of prices. Trial and error will tell you if you have something that is highly desirable priced so low that he is content to work only for enough tokens to buy that item.

Next arrange the reinforcements into a "reinforcement menu." This means listing each reinforcement and its price on a piece of cardboard, paper, etc., just like a restaurant menu. If your child does not have well-developed reading skills, then cut out magazine pictures of the reinforcements and tape them on a piece of paper with their prices written alongside. This helps to show your child what he is earning tokens for. When he wants to cash in some tokens, show him the menu and let him choose his reinforcement.

You will probably find that your child will initially buy things that are immediately consumable—like candy. Once the initial excitement of the system wears off, then you should introduce reinforcements that are not immediately consumable: A trip next week, TV time for the next week, and expensive toy that is bought on "layaway." Many items can be put on a rental basis. By this process and by arranging prices so that your child can't buy everything, you will begin to teach him to act in terms of future consequences—to plan ahead and save for things that are more valuable—and to make decisions among alternatives.

The tangible reinforcements or tokens can be a variety of things: bottle-caps, play money, poker chips, etc. Sometimes we have given a child a notebook and the parent gives points for good behavior. The essential requirement is that the child have something he can see and add up.

At the beginning you will want to check with your child at the completion of every task. You will want to discuss how well the bed was made, what improvements could be made, etc. Then you will award the number of tokens which the job deserves. Remember to reinforce *improvement*; do not wait for perfection.

On the very first day of the program you should pick one area of behavior that your child can do fairly well. As soon as he has completed the job, reinforce him. Then let him choose among several available reinforcements that he can buy with his newly earned tokens and that he can use, eat, play with *right now*. This insures that he will see the relationship between behavior, tokens and reinforcement.

You should establish an exchange time. At first it may need to be every day. Later you will find that your child can wait every other day, then weekly. You will want to consider how many tokens your child can reasonably earn in a week. Remember you are going to be continually raising your standards. You can then adjust prices that will determine how much choice your child will have. You are not doing this to be an unscrupulous merchant. If your child can earn enough tokens to buy everything, he will not have any choices to make. You may also be preparing him for a very unrealistic world. If he cannot possibly earn enough tokens to buy everything, he will have to give real thought to his decisions: to decide whether a candy bar now is more valuable than a trip to the beach next week.

We believe that you will see more "growing-up" in your child in this procedure than you may see anywhere else. This is a major side benefit of this type of program.

As you see your child progressing—mastering the skills you are reinforcing and having a better attitude—you will want to go on and develop new behaviors. The best method is to begin to reduce the number of tokens that can be earned by certain behaviors that have become well-established and introduce new behaviors that are worth more tokens. Again, with these new behaviors, you will start off by reinforcing any improvement and progress toward the desired behavior.

You can reduce the number of tokens earned for "old" behaviors as long as you reinforce "new" ones. This allows your child to continue earning plenty of tokens while learning new behaviors.

Eventually these "old" behaviors will be so well-established that they do not need to be reinforced with tokens. You should then drop out the tokens for them, *but* continue to give social reinforcement for them.

You may also decide that there are some highly undesirable behaviors that you want to eliminate and you wish to do this by taking away tokens when they happen. This can be successful if two rules are followed: (a) Tell your child from the beginning what behaviors will cause him to lose tokens, and how many. You may even wish to put this in writing or post it on his wall chart. But do make sure that this is clear from the beginning. (b) Never let him lose so many tokens that he is "in the hole." This is the surest way to cause a child to lose interest in the whole idea of tokens. When your child has lost tokens, it is a good idea to have some things in mind for him to do to earn some tokens back. This gives you a chance to reinforce him for good behavior after he has been punished for bad behavior.

Also in *both* taking away and giving tokens, remember that the power of tokens lies in the personal interaction between parent and child. Make sure that the exchange is personal—do not get into the habit of dropping tokens in your child's bank or marking them on a chart after your child has finished a task and has left the scene.

SPECIAL TECHNIQUES

At first glance, a token program might seem very complicated. It does not have to be that way, especially if you follow some special techniques that we have discovered the hard way—through our own mistakes.

The first basic technique is to pick as reinforcements only those things that you can both *present* and *withhold*. You should choose reinforcements that can be earned *only* through the token system. If they are available for free outside the program, you cannot expect your child to work to buy them. Also if your child is earning the right to participate in a family outing, be sure that you can really *not* deliver that outing if he does not earn enough tokens.

You may experiment to see if tokens or points work better with your child. Whatever you use, make sure that these tangible symbols of exchange cannot be acquired outside the program. We once made the mistake of using poker chips at a residential facility for the retarded. We had to find new tokens when the worst behavior problem boy always seemed to have a large supply of tokens/poker chips after a weekend at home.

Make sure there is a large enough supply of reinforcements to keep your child interested. We have run across children who hoarded their tokens mainly due to a lack of interest in the reinforcements we had to offer. When they had 500 tokens stashed away, the reinforcing power of five tokens for making their bed was not too great.

Generally any activity can be a reinforcement if enough parental involvement is put into it. If parents are excited about an activity, no matter how small, it is a rare child who does not catch the same excitement.

We have found in all successful programs that the vital force behind tokens is the interaction between adults and children. Tokens as we have said before are a means of pinpointing behaviors in order to allow the parent or teacher to use his reinforcing ability most effectively. We have found that these programs begin to fall down when the human element becomes detached from the tokens. When acceptable behavior becomes commonplace, it still must receive *some* attention; if not, then attention begins to follow only the unusual behavior—the undesired. If you find that as the program goes along, the point awarding and exchange has become routinized and nonpersonal, then immediately reintroduce the human element. Tokens are only as good as the interest and enthusiasm you put into them.

CASE HISTORY I

Terry, age nine, has been home on summer vacation for one month and his mother now believes this will truly be "an endless summer." The days seem to flow together in a continuous pattern. Every morning Terry is up at dawn. He splashes some water on his face, zips a moistened but "unpasted" toothbrush across his teeth and passes a comb over his hair. He tosses his pajamas on the floor, pulls on his clothes and flips a bed cover over a tangled pile of blankets.

He bolts down a few spoonfuls of cereal, drinks half of the milk he doesn't spill out of his glass and flies out the door (loud slam!) for a day of baseball, bicycle riding, uprooting forests, etc.

While Mrs. Smith likes to see her son enjoying himself, she is about to give up hope of getting him to learn to wash, brush his teeth, comb his hair, make his bed, eat his breakfast, etc.

How would you go about setting up a token program to handle this problem? We have outlined the steps below—try filling in the actual program.

1. List as specifically as possible the general things you want Terry to do. How often?
2. Specify where Terry is now in all those behaviors and describe in some detail what terminal behavior should be—what's a properly made bed, etc.
3. Decide what the starting point is in each area. What will be acceptable behavior that you will reward? Cereal half

finished before leaving, three quarters finished? Hair combed better than before, but not necessarily perfect.
4. Rank the behaviors in order of their importance to you, or decide if they are of equal importance.
5. Assign a daily quota of tokens—more tokens for the most important areas.
6. How could you make a visible record of his performance? Wall chart, etc.
7. What reinforcements will you use? Hint—Being able to play outside when finished seems to be pretty powerful—could he rent his baseball equipment, etc?
8. Decide what to use as tokens, when they are to be given, etc., how many he needs to get outside, etc.

INDEX

A
Academics; 181–194
Adult Cues; see Reinforcement
Adult Reinforcement; see Reinforcement
Alphabet; 182, 183

B
Ball Playing; 176–180
Behavior; xi, 5, 11–28, 48, 51, 102
  Analyzing; 12, 83, 122, 128, 132, 139, 146, 147, 148, 153, 162, 167, 173, 176, 178, 196
  Big Behavior; 11
  Incompatible; 58
  Pinpointing; 11, 78, 83, 101, 122, 139, 145, 153, 156, 162, 167, 173, 176, 178, 183, 196
  Small Behavior; 11
Behavior Modification; ix, 3
Behavior Problems; xiii, 47–67, 80
Big Behavior; see Behavior
Brushing Teeth; 145–148, also see Hygiene

C
Case Examples;
  Academics; 193, 194
  Behavior Problems; 60, 63, 66
  Dressing; 134, 135, 136
  Eating; 93, 94, 95, 96, 98, 99
  Hygiene; 149, 150
  Toileting; 119, 120
  Tokens; 205, 206
Catching A Ball; see Eye-Hand Coordination
Chaining; 25, 85, also see Reverse Chaining
Charts; 69, 70, 71, 73, 115, 166
Child Cues; see Cues
Child Reinforcement; see Reinforcement
Combing Hair; 148, also see Hygiene
Consequences; 5, 6, 7
Coordination; 166–175
Counting; 187–189
Cues; xi, 5, 29–35, 48, 51, 78, 84, 102, 103, 128, 140, 154, 156, 162, 168, 176, 178, 185, 198
  Adult; 31, 32, 33, 34, 37
  Child; 33
  Exaggerated; 79
  Signals; 5
  Signs; 5
  Verbal; 79

D
Dressing; 121–127, also see Case Examples
Programs; 132–134

E
Eating; 83–100, also see Case Examples
Exaggerated Cues; 79, also see Cues
Expressive Language; 156
Extinction; 88
Eye-foot Coordination; 172
Eye-hand Coordination; 167
  Catching A Ball; 178
  Playing Ball; 176
  Throwing A Ball; 176

F
Fading Reinforcement; see Reinforcement
Feedback; see Reinforcement
Feeding; see Eating

G
Generaized Reinforcement; see Reinforcement

H
Hair Combing; 148
Handicaps; xvi

208   *Isn't It Time He Outgrew This?*

Hand Washing; 139–145, *also see* Hygiene
Hygiene; 138–150, *also see* Case Examples

I

Incompatible Behavior; *see* Behavior
Instructions; 5

L

Language; 151–160
  Expressive; 156
  Receptive; 152

M

Measurement; 68
Motor Development; 161–180, *also see* Eye-Hand Coordination
  Ball Playing; 176–180
  Walking; 162, 163, 164, 165

N

Numbers; 185, 186

O

Overlearning; xvii

P

Parent Training; xii
Pinpointing; *see* Behavior
Praise; *see* Reinforcement
Primary Reinforcement; *see* Reinforcement
Punishment; 5

R

Rate; xi, 74
Receptive Language; 152
Records; 69, 70, 71, 73, 75, 76, 81, 103, 114, 115, 144, 160, 165, 172, 175, 177, 179, 191
Reinforcement; xi, 6, 7, 36–46, 48, 51, 79, 80, 84, 103, 114, 129, 142, 154, 158, 162, 171, 174, 177, 179, 188, 200

  Adult; 37, 41, 42, 43, 80
  Child; 37, 40
  Fading; 43
  Feedback; 5, 7, 36
  Generalized; 40
  Praise; 39
  Primary; 38, 80, 84, 85
  Punishment; 5
  Reward; 55
  Secondary; 39, 85
  Social; 39
  Token; 41, 195, 196, 206
Research; ix
Responses; 5
Reverse Chaining; 27, 100, 122, 128, 145, 184, 187, 192, *also see* Chaining
Reward; 55

S

Secondary Reinforcement; *see* Reinforcement
Self-Help Skills; 78–82
Shoe Tying; 21, 22, 23, 24, 25
Signals; *see* Cues
Signs; *see* Cues
Small Behaviors; *see* Behavior
Special Techniques;
  Academics; 189
  Ball Playing; 176, 178
  Combing Hair; 148
  Coordination; 168, 174
  Counting; 189
  Dressing; 129
  Eating; 91, 93
  Hygiene; 144, 147
  Language; 154, 159
  Motor Development; 163, 168, 174, 176, 178
  Self-Help; 80
  Toilet Training; 116
  Tokens; 204
  Tooth Brushing; 147
  Walking; 163
  Washing Hands; 144
  Writing; 189
Spoon; 83, 86, 92

Index

T

Temper Tantrums; 48, 49, 50, 51, 53, 54, 55, 59, 73
Throwing A Ball; *see* Eye-Hand Coordination
Time-Out; 89
Toilet Training; 69, 101–120, *also see* Case Examples
Tokens; 48, 49, 51, 73, 195–206, *also see* Case Examples
Tooth Brushing; 145

V

Verbal Behavior; *see* Language
Verbal Cues; *see* Cues

W

Walking; *see* Motor Development
Washing; 139–145, *also see* Hygiene
Withdrawing Reinforcement; 53
Writing; 183–190